At His Feet

At His Feet

Donna Milham

At His Feet

By Donna Milham

Copyright © 2014

ISBN-10:0-692-31732-5
ISBN-13:978-0-692-31732-7

Constant Hope Publishing
PO Box 2344, Evanston, WY 82931
307-679-2616 / www.besharpproductions.com

Cover Artwork: *"Extravagant Love"* By Judy Johnson *(gentlemomentsstudio.com)*
Photographer: Andrea Van Boven Madden *(Multifacetedblog.net)*

ENDORSEMENTS

Our dear friend, Donna Milham has written a beautiful work on true spiritual worship and awakening in its purest form! She has a very unique and creative style of writing, which you will enjoy! Intermixed with poetry, prose, praise and the Word of God, Donna leads you into that tender exchange that takes place between the worshiper and the Worshiped, until our hearts are completely intermingled with His with no desire to turn back! She takes you before His feet, into the depths of extravagant whole-hearted worship of the One we love. As you read you'll feel yourself being brought into the very fire of His love; and, you'll be moved into the place of heartfelt worship of the One who alone is worthy, the magnificent God of all! You'll be moved from a place of just beholding His feet to the place of possessing beautiful fiery feet yourself, ready to run wherever He wants to take you.

Brian and Candice Simmons
The Passion Translation
Stairway Ministries
www.stairwayministries.org

Words have the power to engrave on our hearts, images. The words Donna has scribed from her quiet place, paint a picture of extravagant love. *At His Feet* is an invitation to a lifestyle of abandoned worship and love. This call brings the reader face-to-face with Holy Love. Donna shares transparently from her heart's journey. She has discovered the faithful and true love of God, as she has learned to lay her life down at the feet of Jesus. I believe the timeless message in her writings will touch many generations. Donna's life exemplifies the heart of her message. I encourage the reader to find a quiet place and get ready to hear the sound of Love's heartbeat as you open the pages of this book.

Tracee Anne Loosle
Founder/Director; Intrepid Heart Ministries
www.intrepidheart.org

Donna Milham, my dear friend, extravagant lover of God, and creative expression of His love, has written *At His Feet* from a place of true "knowing". Between poetry and prose, we soar *with wings of color and light;* irresistibly drawn by His Love, transcended and transformed by being with Him. Breathe again, hope again. Like the turning of a gemstone, discover fresh realms of revelation in this contemporary devotional - *At His Feet.*

Susan Card
Artist and Co-leader of Advancing Art
MorningStar Ministries
www.morningstarministries.org

What is the smell of Grace? *"Jesus knelt down and began to write in the dirt."* What is the sound of Mercy? *"Woman, where are your accusers?"* What does Hope look like? *"Neither do I condemn you."* And, what of Unconditional Love? Within the pages of Donna Milham's book <u>At His Feet</u>, each one of our senses is allowed to come alive as we pause, lean in and listen to what Heaven is declaring, and gaze upon the beauty of the Eternal. I believe King David said it so eloquently in Psalm 27:4 (MSG) – *"I'm asking God for one thing, only one thing: to live with Him in His house my whole life long. I'll contemplate His beauty; I'll study at His feet."* It is at His feet that Donna has received insight and revelation that is bound to stir the reader's heart to long for another glance, another moment, another taste of the goodness and love of the Father.

Connie V. Scott
Founder/Director, Voice of Hope Ministries
www.vohministries.org
Constant Hope Publishing
www.besharpproductions.com

DEDICATION

This book is dedicated to my sister, Roberta Costa, who went home to be with the Lord on June 13, 2014. This was a suddenly and she is in glory now with the Lord!

Roberta lived a life of reaching out to others in many ways, yet one way that always touched my life again and again – and countless others lives – were the cards she sent with simple, warm, loving thoughts from her heart. I have kept some of those cherished keepsakes in a box with memories of our lives together.

I miss those envelopes in my mailbox and the joy of what might be inside.

May this book be like an envelope in your mailbox, filled with the joys of my heart from my time with the Holy Three – Father, Son and Holy Spirit!

I pray that you will experience a heart encounter with the Lord, who delights in you!

ACKNOWLEDGMENTS

I would like to thank my family, my dear friends, and my team and tribe for all of your prayers, support, and encouragement.

I am eternally grateful to the One Who is worthy to be praised for His guidance, His grace, and His loving eternal embrace!

"When you live a life of abandoned love,
Surrendered before the awe of God,
Here's what you'll experience: Abundant life!
Continual protection!
And complete satisfaction!"
Proverbs 19:23 TPT

CONTENTS

INTRODUCTION

This book was written from my heart to the One True God who invited me to come and sit at His Feet, to learn the *art of waiting*, of being still with Him, before Him and to become lost in Him.

This book was the Lord's idea, to share with others what He revealed and spoke to my heart and spirit. I resisted writing this book at times, arguing there is no need for one more book, as I would receive announcements of the most current popular book releases.

Then, I remembered reading a book and how it changed my life and thanking God for the book and the author who wrote it.

I clearly heard Him respond, "Suppose they did not write this book and used the same reason you were giving to Me?" Convicted, I repented and said, "Okay Lord I will write this book for Your pleasure. And should it touch one life, one heart that will be an honor and privilege of sharing *our secret times* together with others."

1

❧ ❧ ❧ ❧ ❧ ❧ ❧ ❧ ❧ ❧

Posturing Ourselves at His Feet

❧ ❧ ❧ ❧ ❧ ❧ ❧ ❧ ❧ ❧

AT HIS FEET

"Mary has discovered the one thing most important by choosing the most excellent place – to sit here at My feet. She is undistracted and I won't take this privilege from her." Luke 10:42 (TPT)

<u>Kiss His Feet</u>

His Feet had not been washed
When she kissed them
She washed them with her tears
Kiss His Feet
Kiss His Feet
With adoration and poured out love
Kiss His Feet
Will you Kiss His Feet and
Will you wash the ones He sends into the house
Feet stained with sins and uncleanness of the world

His Feet walked dusty dung-filled streets
Will you wash the ones I send
Dusty and dirty
Will you kiss them with
My Kiss of Mercy
And wash them clean
With holy love
Set them free
With holy love of Me in you
Flowing
From My Pierced Holy Feet
Through you
Cling – oh Cling
To My Feet
Wrap your arms around

My legs
Pillars of Fire
Burn with desire
Now look into My Eyes
And let a fresh deposit of desire and passion
Go in
From this place
Go out
And pour and wash
In holy love

At His Feet...

The posture of adoration, the posture of a poured out life of worship, of holding nothing back from the One who is worthy of all praise – this is what it means to be at His feet. It is the call to a sacrificial way of life and walk. I call it the Galatians 2:20 lifestyle!

"My old life was crucified with Christ and no longer lives; for I was fully united with Him in His death. And now the essence of this new life is no longer mine, for Christ lives His life through me! My real life is Christ – we live as one! My new life is empowered by the faith of the Son of God who loves me so much that He gave Himself for me, and dispenses His life into mine!" Galatians 2:20 (TPT)

I can think of no other posture that would be more honoring, more loving, or more intimate than at His Feet. These are the Feet of the One who left Heaven and took on the form of man *(Philippians 2)*. He did it for the love and desire of His Promised Bride; to restore us to the place of intimacy as sons and daughters of the Father; to give us access to all that is our Home for Eternity – **NOW** - in the present!

To kiss the Feet of the One who is worthy, the One whose Feet were pierced for you and for me. They dripped of the holy Blood He shed on our behalf that we might become partakers of His Divine Nature, enabling us to walk and live in the reality of the full atoning work of His costly sacrifice.

I meditate on this and I run to His Feet. I drop to the ground in adoration – whether it is an actual physical position or within my heart; I fall to the ground in awestruck wonder. What love is this – Divine, Holy, Sacred – who else would ever love me like this?

I hear the heart-cry of Jesus echo through time, *"No one will ever love you like I love you."* This passionate King, this romantic Lover, this burning One with eyes and heart of fiery desire - Who can resist Him? Who would want to? I melt at His Feet in silent worship, clinging tightly to the nail pierced Feet. Rays of Glory Light radiate from the piercings, drawing me into the sacrificial love call – *"All I have is Yours - all I am is because of You…here I am."*

He woos me up the mountain of worship and invites me to lay my very being on the altar of worship, as a dove – a living sacrifice – eyes only for Him. A dove has no peripheral vision, they can only see straight ahead; what is right in front of them. So, with eyes set on His Love, I gladly lay all of my life and love on this altar of worship. Here I encounter Him, His fiery love that overtakes and consumes me; and rising out of the ashes, an eagle now soars with Him in the highest heights, on His very Breath.

The eyes of my heart now see as He sees - heaven's perspectives becoming mine. Each glimpse is being imparted into my being – transforming my views, my ways, my thoughts – I am seeing from His Kingdom reality. I soar with Him in great joy and anticipation of Divine Possibilities – Divine Potential – Divine Designs for my life.

Yes, a laid down lover's call leads to the upward journey with Him into the heights and depths and width and breadth of His Love. Heaven presents a path filled with endless creative opportunities before me, before you. The question remains, will we enter in, will we embark on this journey, and will our response be, *"Yes!"*?

LET HER ALONE
JOHN 12:1-8

Jesus' declaration, made in that room, over that lover still echoes throughout time. And, He continues to declare it over all who worship Him, love Him, sit at His Feet, and wash them with their love and adoration.

Religious busyness and those driven, consider this a waste of time, a waste of resources, and a waste of energy and focus.

Heaven rejoices, angels are astounded, and those in the balcony of heaven who have gone before us, cheer us on, *"Stay in that posture – for that is the posture of true success, true love, and true identity."*

We were created to worship, for worship, and to love and be loved – His Kingdom is Love! Jesus is Love! The atmosphere of our Eternal Home is Love! The Father wants us to live in that atmosphere now, for we are eternal beings now!

"Your kingdom come, Your will be done – we are calling down Love – for Love Himself laid down His life that we might live forever in the Father's Divine Embrace."

Here we become one with Jesus, and live inside of His heart as He lives inside the Father's Heart – embraced by the Holy Three – wrapped in Eternal Security!

What love is this?

Extravagant! And, when Heaven sees extravagance released on earth, it declares –

LEAVE HER ALONE!

EMBRACED BY DIVINITY

"Afterwards one of the Jewish religious leaders named Simon asked Jesus to his home for dinner. Jesus accepted the invitation and went to Simon's home and took His place at the table. In the neighborhood there was an immoral woman of the streets, known to all as a prostitute, who heard about Jesus being in Simon's house. Taking with her an exquisite flask made from alabaster, filled with the most expensive perfume, she went right into the home of the Jewish religious leader, and knelt down at the feet of Jesus in front of all the guests! Broken and weeping, she covered His feet with her long hair. Over and over she kissed Jesus' feet, and then she opened her flask and anointed His feet with her costly perfume as an act of worship!

When Simon the Jewish religious leader saw what was happening, he thought to himself, "This man can't be a true prophet! If He were really a prophet He would know what kind of sinful woman is touching Him!" Jesus spoke up and said, "Simon, I have a word for you." Go ahead, Teacher, I want to hear it, he answered. It's a story about two men who were deeply in debt. One owed the bank $100,000 and the other only owed $10,000. When it was obvious that neither of them would be able to repay their debts, the kind banker very graciously wrote off the debt and forgave them all that they owed. Tell me, Simon — which of the two debtors would be the most thankful? Which one would love the banker most?

Simon answered; I suppose it would be the one with the greatest debt forgiven. You're right, Jesus agreed. Then he spoke to Simon about the woman still weeping at His feet. Don't you see this woman kneeling here? She is doing for Me what you didn't bother to do. When I entered your home as your guest, you didn't think about offering Me water to wash the dust off My feet. Yet she came into your home and washed My feet with her many tears, and then she dried My feet with her hair. You didn't even welcome Me into your home with the customary kiss of greeting, but from the moment I came in, she has not sopped kissing My feet. You didn't take the time to anoint my head and feet with fragrant oil, but she anointed My feet with the finest perfume. She has been forgiven of all her many sins. This is why she has shown Me such extravagant love. But the one who assumes they have very little to be forgiven will love me very little.

Then Jesus said to the woman at His feet, Your sins are all forgiven! But all the dinner guests began to say among themselves, Who is the One who can even forgive sins? Then Jesus said to the woman, Your faith in Me has given you life! Now you may leave and walk in the ways of peace." Luke 7:36–50 (TPT)

This is the picture of Jesus that Luke painted on the canvas of our hearts – revealing the posture of a woman who has been embraced by Divinity, and expresses her heart of thanksgiving to the One who she loves. He reveals the posture of the One who is the recipient of such an extravagant display of adoration – for she did not pour out some of the costly perfume, nor come with a half empty vial, she came with a FULL vial and poured it all out on Him. She wasted her all on Him. Was it waste? Not wasted in the sense that we would talk about wasting our money on foolishness, though the religious in that room who could NOT SEE, saw only waste. Jesus and Heaven, and those who could SEE, to them this was not wasteful, but extravagance!

She was a woman of the streets, a prostitute – one that people back then *(and today)* despised - looked down upon – including those who were her *customers*. Were there any in the room that day? It does not say – **a question to ponder.** Or, were there those who looked *twice, perhaps three times?* They may not have *tasted of her wares,* but perhaps imbibed in their vain imaginations – **a question to ponder.**

It says she HEARD about Jesus being in Simon's house. She was the uninvited guest. She had no invitation – no name to drop – no money to pay anyone to let her in – no name tag or business card – no ministry affiliation – she was a woman of the streets, who HEARD! She had postured herself to listen – to hear. Her broken, lonely, isolated, rejected, self-loathing heart was postured to hear words of HOPE and FUTURE. *"Surely there must be more to life than this life I am living!"*

What did she HEAR? What were the reports? Did she hear of the Roman officer's servant? What stories were being told? Did she hear how he healed the broken hearted and diseased bodies, and that their sins were forgiven?

Hope had somehow been released for her to push through the obstacles of her day and the mark on her life; the scorn and disgust and rejection. She pushed through the looks and the comments and focused only on ONE THING – ONE PERSON – the ONE who was able – able to forgive. This One, who carried the Heart of the Father and of Heaven – the God of the 1st, 2nd, 3rd, 4th, and 5th chance…All who call upon the Name of the Lord - this ONE!

She did not come with a Tupperware container, an old wineskin, a used wooden bowl; she came with an exquisite flask made from alabaster, and as I had stated earlier, it was FILLED with the *most* expensive perfume – **Extravagance** - nothing skimpy about this! This was her all – her best – everything she had she brought with her; her present, her past, and her future were in this flask. She held back NOTHING! Not one part, not one drop of her life or existence, both in the pouring of the bottle or in the posture of her heart and life before Him was withheld. She gave all!

She went right into the home of Simon. She did not ask permission. She was not invited – she just quietly walked into the room. This was not a woman who would be listened to; you would not engage in conversation with her. She was a prostitute – untouchable and unclean. She had no place in the community. She was virtually homeless, because she did not belong anywhere, to anyone.

She entered the room unannounced and knelt down. I do not believe for one minute that she even looked around the room. I believe she entered, taking all the courage she had, knowing the familiar looks and comments. They tormented her day and night, both in reality and in the loneliness of her moments when there were no *clients* – the enemy was relentless in screaming into her ears *who she was* and *where she was going* - eternally damned.

But, she pushed past those voices from hell and the voices of earth; the voices of her community, and the faces and voices of the ones in the room. Her focused gaze was upon the One who was the reason she was there. She does not stand, nor sit; not even a word spoken. Our words often cannot even begin to express the depths of our hearts and being – and again, she is not used to being heard - but merely *used*!

She takes the posture of holy adoration. No one has taught her this – it resides within – it is from an abandoned heart that has no other hope, no one else to turn to, and no one else who would love and accept her. She knelt down at His Feet in front of everyone in the room.

Everyone stops. There is for a moment, silence…Stunned. *"Who is this woman? Who let her in - how did she get in here? The presumption! We need to get her out of here. Why is she with Jesus? How does she know Him? Who does she think she is? Does He know who is touching Him? How can He be a prophet? How could He be the Messiah?* **Impossible!** *Perhaps HE is one of her clients?"*

The beauty of His Holiness is not afraid to let this one who is *unclean* touch Him; for that which is within Him is greater than that which is within her, and will actually consume, overtake, and impart to her that which He walks and lives in. He does not move, He does not reject her; but He looks, He allows, He lets her be who she needs to be right then and there, in broad view of all in that room. Without apology, in the silence of the moment, He sits and receives. I think perhaps in His Heart there is a great smile - perhaps it is on His Face. I know for sure, His Face to her was not stern, but filled with tenderness, love, and grace - giving her worth with His eyes of holy love.

She was broken; weeping, she had come to the end of herself and now she is in an ENCOUNTER with the ONE MAN, who would not touch her in any way that was unholy, who would not look at her with eyes of lust, who would not use her nor abuse her, but who would give her value and worth. She poured out every broken moment at His Feet, every *client* being consumed as she poured out her tears; covering His Feet with her tears and wiping them with her hair. Each memory being consumed - as far as the east is from the west – erased, swallowed up in LOVE - Forgiveness.

Page after page was torn from the journals of her heart – never to be brought before her again by Heaven, by Jesus, by the Father, or by the Spirit. Man perhaps, but not from the Holy Three. She stayed at His Feet a long time, tears flowing. I believe each tear brought a healing and cleansing of her past. Over and over, she kissed Jesus' Feet. Over and over, and over and over! I wondered if those in the room thought, *"When will this end? How long will this go on?"*

How long will that person stay on the floor, out in the Spirit? What possibly could be taking place? Why does that person twirl and twirl in dance, around and around - is that not monotonous? Why does that worship leader sing holy, holy, holy, holy? Does he or she not know anything else? Why does that woman cry so hard and so long - will the tears ever stop? Why is that one raising their hands?

That was me, when I was first saved. I was brought aside by some of the women - they tapped me on the shoulder in chapel. *"We are waiting for you in our room, to meet and talk with you."* I thought I was safe. I had never been to a woman's retreat. I went, wondering what to expect. To my shock, what had been hidden in their hearts and whispered behind my back came forth in a gush, in a moment in that room.

"Who do you think you are raising your hands and standing up in worship? Do you think you are better than us?" I was stunned! There was more, but those words rang out and filled the room, and sought to enter my heart like a knife to kill the very place of extravagant devotion to the One I was so thankful to - to finally be loved and accepted. I could only think to myself, *"If you knew who I was and what He set me free from, you would stand also… And, if you were truly in worship, you would not be watching me and what I was doing. You would be lost in Him, as I seek to be when I come to worship corporately. I stand in honor of the One who set me free and who loves me, not to impress anyone. I stand, because He is the One who I stand for, no man - only Him. I raise my hands in glad surrender, because He is the only One I trust to surrender my life to fully; the only ONE who loves me like He does. Why not extravagantly display my love?"*

Like David, I will be even more undignified than this! You have seen nothing yet! As crazy as I was in the world, with extravagant displays of devotion to things that were not worthy of my love or expressions, I will pour out ALL. I will bring MY FULL extravagant vial and hold back nothing. For HE says I am beautifully and wonderfully made; and so that which HE says, I am! I bring to Him and before Him, and I pour it all out; knowing He will fill me again with more love. And then,

I will pour that out. It is the Eternal Dance of my heart with His Heart - pour in, pour out, pour forth, fill – pour out, pour forth – fill.

There she is pouring out her all; crying and drying off His Feet. She opens her flask and anoints His Feet with her costly perfume - **AN ACT OF WORSHIP!**

To live our lives in ACTS OF WORSHIP, flowing from hearts abandoned before Him; to show the world HE IS WORTHY; to not be ashamed in the hidden place, or in the city square -- we will pour out! WHO WILL POUR OUT their hearts and lives of devotion unashamed? No blushing here - holy, holy, holy moments, in HIS PRESENCE.

The fragrance fills the room - surrounds Jesus - surrounds her - begins to surround those in the room. Conviction - is there conviction or just condemnation?

When the oil begins to flow and people respond around us, do we sit and judge from not understanding? Or, do we smell the fragrance and enter into His presence. HE IS HERE. The anointing is here. THE ONE we are waiting for has just entered. OPEN WIDE OUR SENSES HOLY SPIRIT to know when HE has come, when YOU have come; and to fall at His Feet and worship. In a gathering, in the marketplace, in the square; in the supermarket, on the beach, or on the streets – it does not matter – only that He comes!

It is interesting; those into *new age* and worshipers of false gods have no hindrances in displaying their *devotion* to their false gods. I see them on the beach, in the parks, in the woods, on cliffs, on mountains, in valleys, and in the squares. Where do we stand as God's people – where is our display of devotion for those to see, experience, and enter into the fragrance that we are to carry everywhere we go?

I wonder if perhaps, this is what Heaven is waiting for? Your Kingdom come and Your will be done on earth, as it is in Heaven. I realize that is multifaceted, but for this context I believe Heaven is looking for a people of extravagant devotion – those who are not ashamed to worship in the light of the day, in the middle of the crowd - to display the glories of the One, through worship.

Acts of worship! I wonder if Jesus came to a public place today, who would kiss His Feet with their tears and wipe them with their hair, and pour forth their all?

"When Simon the religious leader SAW what was happening, he thought to himself, 'This man can't be a true prophet if He were really a prophet He would know what kind of sinful woman is touching Him. Jesus spoke up and said, "Simon I have a word for you." Luke 7:39 (TPT)

Jesus read Simon's thoughts – had a word of knowledge – the Spirit of God allowed Him to have knowledge of his thoughts and heart intent. In front of the whole room, Jesus spoke a word to him that would challenge and expose the condition of each person's heart and thoughts in that room.

"It's a story about two men who were deeply in debt. One owed the bank $100,000 and the other only owed $10,000. When it was obvious that neither of them would be able to repay their debts, the kind banker very graciously wrote off the debt and forgave them all they owed. Tell me, Simon – which of the two debtors would be the most thankful? Which one would love the banker most?'

Simon answered, 'I suppose it would be the one with the greatest debt forgiven!'

'You're right Simon', Jesus agreed. Then he spoke to Simon about the woman still weeping at His feet.

Don't you SEE this woman kneeling here? She is doing for ME what you didn't bother to do. When I entered your home as your guest, you didn't' think about offering Me water to wash the dust off My feet. Yet she came into your home and washed My feet with her many tears and then she dried My feet with her hair. You didn't' even welcome Me into your home with the customary kiss of greeting but from the moment I came in, she has not stopped kissing My feet. You didn't take time to anoint my head and feet with fragrant oil, but she anointed My feet with the finest perfume. She has been forgiven of all her many sins. This is why she has shown Me such extravagant love. But the one who assumed they have very little to be forgive will love me very little." Luke 7:41-47 (TPT)

"Simon, what do you SEE?" This is the great question of the moment! "Do you really SEE this woman who is kneeling HERE? DO YOU SEE her displays of Love and devotion? Do you SEE she has held nothing back and given her ALL? **DO you see SHE IS DOING FOR ME WHAT YOU DIDN'T BOTHER TO DO?"**

"SHE came into your home and WASHED MY FEET with her many tears. You didn't even wash them with water, as our custom says to do. SHE THEN dried My Feet with her hair. You didn't wash and you didn't dry them with a towel, or offer me water or a towel. You didn't give me the customary kiss of greeting, but from the moment she came into the room, SHE HAS NOT STOPPED KISSING MY FEET."

Kissing MY FEET – they were not cleaned of the dust, dirt, and soiling of the animal strewn streets. She did not wait until MY FEET were clean – SHE just began to Kiss them.

Just as I do not wait for those I came to seek and save to be CLEAN before I embrace them, touch them, eat with them, love them, and set them free. I receive them just as they are – with the dust and dirt and filth of their lives, from living in this sin-filled world. I wash them clean with forgiveness from Father's Heart through mine into theirs.

She kisses My Feet again and again and again…and I kiss those I love, again and again and again. I kiss their hearts with forgiveness, with grace, with future and a hope, with worth and value, with sonship, and with kisses of Eternity and their Eternal Home.

"You didn't take time to anoint My head and feet with fragrant oil, but SHE anointed MY feet with the FINEST perfume – HER BEST. SHE HAS BEEN FORGIVEN OF ALL HER MANY SINS - THIS IS WHY she has SHOWN ME such EXTRAVAGANT LOVE. But the one who assumes they have very little to be forgiven, will love very little."

Never forget who you were when He found you. I am not a sinner saved by grace any longer. I was - I am now a son/daughter, who is loved and loves extravagantly in return. The ONE who came and washed me and poured the costly sacrifice of His Life – His Blood – EVERY DROP; He did not hold back ONE DROP OF HIS BLOOD FOR ME. With every drop, HE EMPTIED HIMSELF FOR ME. How can I not pour forth MY ALL for HIM - every drop of my life, my heart, my love, my song, my devotion, my dreams, my desires - ALL FOR HIM AND ON HIM - and display it in public, if that is His desire to live FOR HIM FROM THIS LOVE?

He poured out HIS ALL for ME! That speaks, shouts, declares into all eternity MY WORTH – MY VALUE – MY IDENTITY! It laughs in the face of worthlessness, shame, low self-esteem, and an orphan heart and spirit. It swallows up homelessness, identity loss, and the questions, "Who am I?" and, "Why am I here?" It releases dignity, royal posture, hope, and confidence in Whose we are and who we are. This is our destiny – this is our journey – this is what we were created for, and will always be – AT HIS FEET! Now and forever - while we are about His Business, within our hearts, we are At His Feet.

We do not presume upon our life's journey; we walk intimately with Him in the posture of listening, waiting, and worshiping. He whispers and He looks into our eyes and says, "You have chosen the best! You are not wasting your time. You have indeed found the very reason of your existence – why WE created you – intimacy, intimate fellowship, holy dialogue with the Holy Three – you have found the very purpose of your life; and from this place, all the blessings of Heaven will unfold around you, into you, and before you. Your faith in Me has given you life! NOW, you may leave and walk in the ways of peace."

Not one day, or someday, but NOW, walk in the ways of peace! The One who is Peace, released Peace and says, "NOW, THIS DAY, walk in peace. PEACE, from the place of knowing I have received you and embraced you and your extravagant love. You are Mine, now walk in the peace of knowing WHOSE you are and let us walk this journey together in intimate exchange - Heaven is within your heart - listen, hear My whisper and rest in My Peace!"

And so I stood, hands raised, I did not stop - I would not be silenced. I went that next Sunday, and I stood – not out of defiance, nor to prove my point – I went to worship. Is that not why the doors were opened to that church building? Were not the doors of Heaven opened and we were given access to *come up here*? And so, I accessed with the rights and privileges of one who had been darkness and was now light.

Of one who did not belong, and now was Divinely owned and loved.

Of one who had been an orphan, and was now a daughter.

Of one who had lived a life of my own choosing and filled with sin, now laid down at His Feet…

So, I stood and today, I still stand - without apology. I raise my hands, I dance, I cry, I shout, I rejoice, I spin, I leap, I fall down at His Feet, and I pour my all out on Him!

Will you join me, will you join with Heaven?

LEAVE HIM ALONE

A cry came from a friend - he had just been judged for his dance. He was crying on the phone. I heard the rejection down to the depth of his being. These were gut wrenching judgments! His whole being accused of who he was NOT - put before a committee, or supposedly those in the *know* of reading a person's spirit…called discernment. My understanding of discernment from God is He brings forth light and life; future and hope to the darkest and most hopeless places. It does not cause one to stumble out of a room, barely able to breathe. In fact, the very life breath of God was not in the room at all; instead the accusations of hell filled the room with toxicity – the pointing fingers. I could hear hell screaming. I could hear Heaven's Declaration in that moment over him – **LEAVE HIM ALONE!**

I remember it hit me like a lightning bolt as I sat in my car at Shaw's Supermarket. The phone rang as I was getting out of the car. I stopped to answer and heard the desperate cries of a brother in need. I can still hear it, and feel the Thunder of Jesus' Voice – *"LEAVE HIM ALONE"* was being declared over him in the Spirit realm. I opened wide my mouth and declared it over him. I painted the picture of the woman who anointed Jesus, and Jesus declared the same to those around her.

And so, IT ECHOES through time – for what can stop the Words of Jesus – then or now? What He declares is eternal! *"Let there be…"* (Genesis 1) is still creating worlds and galaxies. The astronomers believe they have discovered new galaxies they couldn't see before, but in reality they were never there. His Word is creating worlds; and recreating men's hearts with Holy Love and Light.

LET THERE BE – LEAVE HER ALONE – LEAVE HIM ALONE

Creative Release – healing and guarding words of Divine Creation and Divine Protection!

We posture ourselves in and under His Words – His Decrees, and we let them hover and brood over and impart into us the very substance of His DNA. Here we are changed. They are like a cloud over us – stay in the shelter of the Living Words from the One Who is the Living Word! His Words, Creating life within us – let there be life!

My friend began to breathe in the creative healing release, the guarding words of a Lover, of a Father who heard and saw it all, and had something to say from Heaven. His Decrees swallowed up the decrees of man and their opinions. *LEAVE HIM ALONE* - Holy Keeping – Holy God – Holy Love – what love is this! Perfect love casts out all fear!

THE SOUNDS OF WATERS WASHING

Washed by the Blood of Jesus
Washed daily in the Water of His Word
Reading before Him, with Him, the Word - it washes
Waiting in His Presence – it washes over and in and through
Cleansing, ever cleansing – mind, thoughts, attitudes, judgments,
sickness of soul and body – washing out

Light in darkness
Lights in the darkness
We are meant to walk as holy luminaries
Swords of brilliant holy light
Canvases of lightning displaying His Radiance
Shattering darkness with every step
Steps of light in streets of darkness

Holy luminaries
Walking out holy highways
Making way – showing the way – to His Kingdom
His Throne of Holy Light, Life and Love

2

Holy Eyes of Justice

EYES OF THE LION & THE LAMB

"Jesus returned to the Mount of Olives, but early the next morning he was back again at the Temple. A crowd soon gathered, and he sat down and taught them. As he was speaking, the teachers of religious law and the Pharisees brought a woman who had been caught in the act of adultery. They put her in front of the crowd. "Teacher," they said to Jesus, "this woman was caught in the act of adultery. The Law of Moses says to stone her. What do you say?" They were trying to trap him into saying something they could use against him, but Jesus stooped down and wrote in the dust with his finger. They kept demanding an answer, so he stood up again and said, "All right, but let the one who has never sinned throw the first stone!" Then he stooped down again and wrote in the dust. When the accusers heard this, they slipped away one by one, beginning with the oldest, until only Jesus was left in the middle of the crowd with the woman. Then Jesus stood up again and said to the woman, "Where are your accusers? Didn't even one of them condemn you?"

"No, Lord," she said. And Jesus said, "Neither do I. Go and sin no more." John 8:1-11 (NLT)

Hear the sound of governmental authority, the steps of the Lion of Judah resounding with the authority of Heaven. The reason He was sent, the reason He willingly came – to reveal Home.

"The Spirit of the LORD is upon me, for he has anointed me to bring Good News to the poor. He has sent me to proclaim that captives will be released, that the blind will see, that the oppressed will be set free, and that the time of the LORD's favor has come." Luke 4:18-19 (NLT)

Here He was representing His mandate and mission from Heaven. What was deemed before the foundations of the earth – Jesus Christ – Savior – Redeemer of mankind – revealed! Now, standing in this courtyard which had suddenly become a courtroom; Justice and Mercy Himself would be the Judge, Advocate, and Council. Heaven watched. Angels poised and ready; He was constantly in tune with Father, and knew this was a moment to reveal Heaven and His Father's Heart!

Footsteps of the Lion – confident, ruling, and full of Divine authority; the One who created Heaven and earth, stars and seas, wonders of the galaxies, stooped to the ground that He spoke into existence, and wrote in the sand. The One, who wrote the 10 Commandments for His people, with His very Finger! The One, who wrote of the sin of adultery – this same Finger writing now!

"When the Lord finished speaking with Moses on Mount Sinai, he gave him the two stone tablets inscribed with the terms of the covenant, written by the finger of God." Exodus 31:18 (NLT)

Divine Finger of authority – Right forefinger of His Right Hand, equals Prophet/Faith/Authority – Right Hand of God. All power - All glory - All honor to Him. He directs kings and kingdoms, commands angel armies; and this Finger writes what is on the Father's Heart! Hear the Sound of Mercy - Slow and deliberate – declaration being made.

See the angry, murderous, self-righteous mob; hypocrites, self-serving, demonically influenced; legalistic, religious, pious, and filled with murder and hatred.

This woman caught in the act of adultery, how did she end up here? Was she abandoned? An orphan, abused, raped, or was she simply a woman who had no other way to survive, a widow? What happened? It does not say. Labels – so quick we can label and judge and become like the crowd. Our stones are our words!

The lie we believed as kids, "Sticks and stones may break my bones, but words can never hurt me!" **WRONG!** Words, like stones, do kill – not the flesh, but they crush hearts, kill dreams, break relationships, end destinies, and release curses and shame. And, we are accountable for every idle word we speak.

In the eyes of this mob, there is no love, but simple hatred, human justice, and the letter of the law - legalism. God's Government is relational. The woman is caught in adultery – how can we bring her to the revelation of the wrong done, heal the root cause, restore and heal, and bring her into her future and hope? This is the question Heaven asks.

"For God so loved the world..." *(John 3:16)* - The answer resounding through time.

These are the eyes the woman saw as she prepared to be stoned to death. She was alone, no one to help her. Shouts, accusations, anger, dust, rocks - in moments she would die a painful and agonizing death of humility, worthless, hated, and abused - alone! Scenes of her life flashing before her, like when someone is drowning – childhood memories – perhaps of her playing in a field, her mother cooking, sleeping safely in bed – mother and father - home. Oh, to be young again – a little girl safe, but suddenly she hears the roar of anger again. This is her reality, and her life is about to come to an end. Where is help? There is none. Who will save her? She sees no one! The law will be enforced and she will be stoned to death.

Not the man – only she would be killed – what of the man? Was he married, single, a leader, a teacher, a businessman – who was he? It does not say – but he too was guilty. This was injustice in great display; injustice that is still alive today.

Heaven sees and begins to display its glory. Hear the sound of Conviction! Jesus writes in the sand – slow and deliberately He writes – one at a time, the rocks begin to drop. Conviction – Guilty!

Heaven hears – the earth hears – the woman hears the sound of the rocks. Her tensed body awaited the deadly blows. Feeling nothing, she unfolds from her fetal posture of preparing to die, and saw what her heart could not believe. The rocks were dropped out of the murderous hands – they fell to the ground - the sting of death fell with them. For the One, Who would soon conquer death, hell, and the grave was there in that moment representing the Holy Three – Father, Son, Holy Spirit and their Kingdom!

Death sentence rolled up like a scroll. Gavel in Heaven struck! There would be no death today; hell would not celebrate, nor receive another soul.

I am sure as she looked out into the crowd of angry men, there were other *clients* there – those who had used her services for their pleasures, and yet could in a moment stone her to death. Why? Because she was nothing – LABELED NOTHING! It would be easier to stone a *nothing*, than a *somebody*. She was of no value, no worth, no contribution to society except to fulfill a man's fantasies and desires. It was easy for them to Murder her – kill the evidence – kill the one, who had the proof of who were actually her *clients*.

Even to this day, when a prostitution ring is broken up, how often are the clients and ringleaders exposed? Whose pictures are normally shown – who takes the heat and brunt of it?

See His Eyes of Justice, THE LAMB, Who came to save ALL of mankind – Shepherd of His Sheep. His Eyes of Justice burn with righteousness, holiness, and truth – this is WHO HE IS – the Righteous One – Holy One – He is TRUTH – HE is JUSTICE – HE is MERCY!

Mercy triumphs over judgment...

Mercy confronted judgment that day – Face to face showdown. One Kingdom against another!

Eyes Ablaze with Jealous Love – Love stood that day – Covenant Love – staring down and facing demons of darkness, lewdness, hatred, evil, sensuality, and RELIGION! The Eyes that would be filled with Blood from the Crown of Thorns on His Head – redeeming man's thoughts, perceptions, the way He sees, views, thinks, ponders, plans – dripping into Eyes, so we would see as He sees! Cleansing our eye gates, to see with Him – holy eyes – pure eye gates – gateways for Heaven to see through; and men to see Heaven in our eyes and hear it from our mouths, because our thoughts flow from His Mind and Heart within us.

Eyes of Justice - staring into each one's face and eyes – Thud – Thud – Thud – hear the sound of the rocks dropping with conviction. One by one, they leave. The woman still on the ground - afraid – what is happening? Who is this? Will they change their minds and pick up the stones again? This has NEVER happened, always the woman is killed, always the crowd wins – But here she remains – not one stone had come her way! Who – what – what is she to do? Run home, run away – what now?

The Eyes of Justice, Righteous Anger – now look away from her accusers; her would be murderers and look to her. Justice is now soft and embracing.

She did not look up at first for she was clothed in shame, worthless, of no value, an object – No MAN looked into her eyes – EVER – no one looked into her eyes! She was an object for man's lusts. In the market, she was scorned and alone. She was completely devalued - living life alone. Imagine no one looks into your eyes, even as you purchase your food or fetch water. You're ALONE, GOSSIPED ABOUT, and SLANDERED with evil WHISPERINGS.

She keeps her face to the ground and slowly inches her body towards this MAN – this ONE, Who stepped in and saved her. She must thank Him, meet Him, but how? She dare not approach. No man had ever treated her nicely – only abuse – no one touched her warmly – only sensually, and there was NO SAFE PLACE. She was nothing in her own eyes, but her right hand is extended, as she inches her way toward this Man. He watches – He waits – for HE IS SAFETY. He is REDEMPTION. He is FUTURE AND HOPE!

Finally, what seemed like an eternity and yet a moment, She grasps His Feet – she holds on. What does she feel and sense? Moments ago, poised to die – now, she touches the Eternal One, Who IS Peace, Who is Love, Who is Mercy. What does she sense flowing from His Being into hers? I believe she came into the realm of Holy, Eternal, Covenantal Love!

She never knew of this LOVE; never dreamed of this LOVE, but suddenly, she is in a Divine Encounter with the Savior, the Lover of the World!

For God so loved the world...

She touched the Feet that would soon be pierced. Feet of the Lamb, Who would lay down His Life for her – for you and for me – that ALL would have eternal life – now and forever – our sins forgiven, and humanity being restored to relationship with the Father.

The One who stepped down – stepped in *(Philippians 2:5-11)*.

The Feet of the One, Who left Heaven – humbly stepped down from the Throne, became seed in the womb of Mary, and born of a woman; laid aside all Divine power to walk as a man in obedience to the Father, and showed us how to live and walk as sons of God. This One NOW stopped to save her!

Feet that were SAFE – she could cling to, hold onto – she would have been happy to be THERE forever! He was the lighthouse, the safe harbor, the immovable rock of the ages – she clung.

The sound of what He wrote still encircles the spiritual atmosphere. I wonder if she read what He wrote? Did she hear the *thud* of the rocks – echoing – hell screaming, "No, no, no!" - Heaven rejoicing over one soul who finds forgiveness, mercy, and salvation?

She clung to Future and Hope, not knowing WHO He was. But at this moment - **WHO DO YOU SEE?** Who is this woman to you, NOW? While she is on the ground clinging, what is her identity to you? Is she a prostitute, worthless, and not worth your trouble? Is she a possible candidate to share His Love with her, or too far gone? Is she too big of a project? Does she have too much of a past? **WHO IS SHE RIGHT NOW?** Not later, when she tells her testimony and is *cleaned up*, but NOW! For He shed His blood, not only for you and me, but for her and the millions yet to hear! We must SEE AS HE SEES - People's value and worth!

Slowly – painstakingly slow – she looks up and His Eyes are awaiting hers. His Eyes looking intentionally, purposely into hers; Eyes filled with Mercy, Forgiveness, Justice, and Acceptance. One look – eyes locked – she is captured by Holy Love.

Without a word, Holy Light, Love and Life pour – Radiant Beams of Heaven's Love flow into her eyes and her being. WHAT LOVE IS THIS? These Eyes of honor, trust, and safety are Pure Pools of Waters of Love. She feels the safety as she now sees His Right Hand being extended to her - Right Hand of the Father, through the Son – releasing as He extends – ACCEPTED IN THE BELOVED! This was Divine Acceptance – Divine Love. Perhaps the only safe Hand ever extended to her - Hand of Rescue and Redemption - Hand that sought nothing, but gave her everything - Hand that brought value, worth, restoration, love, and safety.

A prostitute transformed in a moment to DAUGHTER, PROMISED BRIDE OF THE LAMB – forever changed!

The pages of her life were turned by the Eternal Hand; now THE NEXT CHAPTER TO BEGIN.

I once was – but now I am...

Forever changed by an encounter with ONE MAN Who wrote in the sand. Sound of Eternal Love, Mercy, and Grace - Extended Hand of Forgiveness - Divine Embrace!

Finally, He speaks, "Where are your accusers, didn't' even one of them condemn you?"

"No Lord."

"Neither do I – go and sin no more."

The One, Who said, "Let there be Light," now speaks to her. Light overcomes darkness. Love overcomes death, hell, and the grave.

43

Her shame removed – she is Divinely Accepted. She is transformed in a moment by Holy Love. There is no hidden agenda in His Heart, only that she is now part of the Kingdom of Heaven.

The Next Chapter – so, what will her life be like from here? She now has a future and a hope, and has encountered Holy Love Himself – forever transformed – in a moment!

When we see someone, will we see as He sees? Will we label, judge, or throw stones with words of judgment and opinions? Will we see as He sees – begin to hear from Heaven, see the Next Chapter, and begin to decree it over their lives?

What is your next chapter? Perhaps you are still living under shame, hearing words like rocks thrown at you – still the sting of them remains - perhaps the scars – people's opinions and judgments holding you prisoner to the past – but, God is a present-future God, Who comes in and in a moment, heals us and sets us free from the torment of *words spoken.* Curses are broken – death sentences of destinies cancelled, and future and hope put in its place!

The Next Chapter God is leading His people into is the absolute assurance of our IDENTITY in Him; to walk in the fullness of this truth. He is after every lie and false perception we have of ourselves, and we have received from others. He wants us to walk in the Truth of His Word and who He says we are!

Jesus knew exactly Who He was, and in John 8:12, begins to declare, "I AM THE LIGHT OF THE WORLD, if you…"

"Jesus spoke to the people once more and said, "I am the light of the world. If you follow me, you won't have to stumble through the darkness, because you will have the light that leads to life." The Pharisees replied, "You are making those claims about yourself! Such testimony is not valid." Jesus told them, "These claims are valid even though I make them about myself. For I know where I came from and where I am going, but you don't know this about me. You judge me by human standards, but I do not judge anyone. And if I did, my judgment would be correct in every respect because I am not alone. The Father who sent me is with me. Your own law says that

if two people agree about something, their witness is accepted as fact. I am one witness, and my Father who sent me is the other."

"Where is your father?" they asked. Jesus answered, "Since you don't know who I am, you don't know who my Father is. If you knew me, you would also know my Father." Jesus made these statements while he was teaching in the section of the Temple known as the Treasury. But he was not arrested, because his time had not yet come." John 8:12-20 (NLT)

As you continue to read this passage, men begin to challenge Jesus and who He was. Their own pride came forth when He said to them, *"I tell you the truth before Abraham was born I AM; and they picked up stones to stone him."* He slips away! Men's hearts can only be changed by an encounter with the Lord!

God is calling us to encounter Him again, this day. He wants to show us the NEXT CHAPTER of our lives; to step fully out of the past and fully into today and our future.

What would He title the Next Chapter of your life? What would you want that Chapter to read?

3

~~~~~~~~~~~

Judah's Jealous Love

~~~~~~~~~~~

WHAT LOVE IS THIS

"Place me like a seal over Your heart or like a seal on Your Arm. For love is as strong as death and its JEALOUSY is as enduring as the grave. LOVE FLASHES LIKE FIRE THE BRIGHTEST KIND OF FLAME. Many waters CANNOT quench love – neither can rivers drown it." Song of Solomon 8:6-7 (NLT)

Love flashes like Fire – the brightest kind of flame. Your Jealous Love - flashing – bright – intense - eyes can barely look because of the intensity of this love! But, by Your grace, You enable us to glance, to even gaze at the brilliance of Your Desire.

Stars in the sky – brilliant, shining, announcing, and declaring JEALOUS LOVE has left Heaven; has disrobed Himself of Divinity and has come naked, vulnerable onto earth as a baby, an infant crying out in holy intercession.

Man, apart from God would only hear a baby's cry, but Heaven and all of creation heard Eternity's Cry. Eternal Love's Cry of Holy Intercession. Cry and Declaration – *Messiah is Born.* And, for the sake of OUR HOLY DESIRE and for the one's WE created; My Father and I, together with Holy Spirit - I came – I have come – HERE I AM - HERE AM I.

It will take eyes and hearts opened by Holy Spirit, to see WHO I AM, to see I AM in a manger. The animals knew. They bowed and sat by gazing at the ONE, WHO spoke them into existence.

First Adam named them, but the Last Adam has flashed upon the scene now. Earth is poised, ready to receive her salvation. It groans in holy response and bows its knees. Will mankind bow? Will mankind see?

The shepherds, lowly in the world's eyes SAW AND HEARD Heaven's Declaration, as Jealous Love Flashed in the sky - Pulsating – Illuminating - Declaring, *"Immanuel, God with us."* They must go – love draws, compels them. Across hills and plains, on a cold wintry night, they arise. They must go and see what – WHO Heaven is announcing. They have no gifts to offer. They are poor and simple shepherds. They have only the posture of bowed knees, of lips to declare praises, of eyes to behold and adore. They have only the gift of themselves; the gift to step away from the daily mandates of their lives, and respond to a sign in the sky.

They didn't have to go. They could have remained on the lowly hillside. Oh, love as strong as death illuminated the sky that night. Eyes and hearts AWAKENED by this Jealous Love, they chose to go. Never regretting as they gazed upon I AM - The One who would stand in the Garden of Gethsemane and speak with holy confidence -

"Who do you seek?"

"Jesus of Nazareth," they responded.

"I AM HE." And, they FELL at His Decree.

Jealous Love - knowing His Time to drink the cup of Eternal Suffering and damnation, STOOD – COMPELLEDY BY HOLY DESIRE – FOR A BRIDE; He could see, smell, and hold down through the corridors of time. And He stood in the face of hell's attempts to quench Love's Rescue, but this was settled. Unshakeable Love that will not stop or quit, that presses through – that looks hell in the face and says, "THEY ARE MINE...you cannot have them. For the ones that will respond to My Heart's Desire, will have written on their hearts and sing from their mouths – *I'M YOURS!*

This will COMPEL them through the valleys of death. This Fiery Flashing Flame of Love will not be quenched! For as they come to Me again and again, I, the Heavenly Billows, blow - blow – blow. I fan the flame of Holy Passion and Desire. I pour in fresh oil as they come aside with Me.

Altars of hearts – flashing brilliant - Men's eyes opened. What is this that just passed by? What is in the EYE of this One before me? I smell smoke. I feel fiery heart. Who – What is this?

50

It is Immanuel. It is the Bridegroom. It was a baby, who is now the Lion Lover, Roaring Over the Earth. *"You Are Mine!"*

THE BABY'S CRY IS NOW THE LION'S ROAR
LUKE 1:12

A baby wrapped snugly in strips of cloth –
The Lion, Who would roar before Lazarus' tomb
"Roll back the stone",
and Decree – COME FORTH,
remove his grave clothes.
Strips of cloth
unraveled now at HIS COMMAND.
no one questioned –
they obeyed.

Flesh awakened – pink again.
Blood purging, rushing, gurgling through Lazarus's veins.
Organs responded -
Heart beating in rhythm with Lion's Decree
COME FORTH.

They unravel the strips of cloth,
Uncovering LOVE'S RESPONSE to hell's grip.
Jealous Love Conquers Death.
Hell MUST let go
At His DECREES.

Baby wrapped snugly in strips of cloth.
Can you hear the SOUND,
As Mary would change His strips of cloth
Prophesying to the earth – to nations – to hell
A DAY IS COMING,
When death will lose its sting,
Hear with each strip of cloth – changing.
The prophetic decree that will be spoken at a tomb one day,
And then at a CROSS on Golgotha's hill.

They took My Robe -
Could not tear it.
This Robe of Justice would not be torn in two.
No, for all ETERNITY, man will see the power of My Robe of Justice!

Torn in two – the veil separating man from ME
Holy Three
Ah, naked I came
Naked I hung
That those I LOVE would be clothed forever
IN MY DESIRE
Hell cannot strip MY BRIDE
I clothe HER with My Very Look, Gaze, Words of Love and Life -
Wrap her in My Decrees of Beauty, Passion, Purity, Purpose,
Value, and Worth.
I wrap her – cover her shame, sorrows and regrets.
I AM future and hope.
I wrap her in dreams of Heaven -
How beautiful are her garments -
Brilliant in COLOR.

Did you see that flash in her heart?
Oh yes – we are ONE – hearts ablaze.
I AM hers and she is MINE.
I hung gladly.
I came willingly.

Strips of cloth – folded neatly in tomb, in garden.
Rolled back stone
Hell couldn't stop that stone being rolled back
Nor the Eternal Sound it released and still releases
He's Alive Forevermore!
Keys - Keys - Keys of LIFE
Conquering King
The baby's cry is now the LION'S ROAR

It was always one and the same.
Eyes to see –
Ears to hear –
Hearts to understand and respond.

4

~~~~~~~~~~~~

Divine Encounters

~~~~~~~~~~~~

AMAZED

"SEE my servant will prosper; He will be highly exalted. Many were AMAZED then they SAW Him – beaten and bloodied so disfigured, one would scarcely know He was a person. And He will AGAIN STARTLE many nations. Kings will stand speechless in His Presence for they WILL SEE what they had not previously been told about and they WILL UNDERSTAND what they had NOT heard about." Isaiah 52:13-15 (NLT)

You startled nations in Bethlehem – Three wise men, shepherds – stood speechless. They SAW and UNDERSTOOD. AMAZED - THE HIGHLY EXALTED ONE came as a baby – returning in Holy Light.

You startled Paul on the Damascus Road. You startled hell when You descended and took the keys, setting captives free. You swallowed up death – shot through realms of the Spirit – DUNAMIS EXPLOSION – RESURRECTION POWER! KEYS – SOUND OF THE KEYS OF AUTHORITY - THE LION, WHO IS THE LAMB!

Baby in the manger with sheep - Shepherd – Perfect Lamb, He had no keys in His tiny fingers.

He was the KEY AND THE DOOR to Eternal Life. He gave Himself willingly, No man took His life. He unlocked death, hell, and the grave.

Jesus – baby in the manger - Eternal Eyes - Beautiful baby… He was unrecognizable on the Cross - Beautiful in Resurrection - Glorious in His Return.

HEAVEN'S RESPONSE

"O Lord, my God, how great You are You are robed with honor and with majesty. You are dressed in a ROBE OF LIGHT." Psalm 104 (TPT)

You took off this Robe – stepped out of Heaven – and stepped into the womb of a handmaiden. The cry on her lips still echoing upon earth; the angels carried her response to Heaven. It echoed there. The stars resounded in brilliant light; the Father rejoiced, *"Salvation's Plan has begun this day!"* This is HEAVEN'S RESPONSE to an OPEN WOMB; A HOLY *YES;* a laid down life. He took off His Robe of Light and became a Seed; stepped into her womb - Eternal Son, a Seed. He was the Seed of Promise for all of man's destinies. Father rejoiced for His children would be HIS again.

But, the Son is gone from Heaven. I wonder what it was like when He vacated His Heavenly Home - angels watching – Holy Spirit hovering over Mary? Even as He did at the command – *Let There Be Light,* from Light Himself – Father of Lights - now, the Son of Light within a woman's womb. John leaped in Elizabeth's womb, for he recognized this Shining One, Who he would prepare the way for - making way for the King of Kings.

Humility abounded that day, causing an Eternal display. To pour into hearts, for each test of pride and self-focus, to gaze upon and fall on our knees - Crying – *only Your Will and Your Way*!

I wonder did the Light within shine from His Eyes? Flashes of lightning escaping here and there; brilliant in what they carried from HOME. The SEED had within HIMSELF all of Heaven - totally dependent on the Father and Spirit.

Holy Three – separated and yet, still ONE...Showing THE WAY to walk in Union and dependency - this Robe of Light, Brilliant, dazzling with Eternity's Pulse of Worship. You are LIGHT – to earth and the Heavens, the Bright Morning Star, Who awakens the dawn.

LIGHT RELEASERS

"The Lord blanketed Egypt in darkness; You Who Are Light awakens our soul."
Psalm 105:28 (TPT)

We cannot of our own inept wisdom think we are wise enough or smart enough to find YOU. No – You draw – You woo. You draw back the blanket of darkness over our souls and captivity. And, You awaken our spirit with the Holy Light of Revelation. Holy Spirit fanning the rays of Truth and Light into our very being that we might hear, see, understands, and choose. Veils of darkness over minds; who will lift the veil? Where are the Sons of Light - praying, going, and releasing Holy Light and Truth, so others can choose Eternal Life and Light?

Veil Lifters – arise!

Light Releasers – shine!

Let there be Light and Life!

For all those who sit in the shadow of death, Behold a LIGHT has come! It is in you and me...the babe in a manger, NOW the Eternal King - Reigning. Death has lost its sting for Sons of Light. Dawn Awakeners – lift the veil of darkness and night with song and sounds; moves and decrees of Light! Open wide your mouths and see its release - Words of Mercy, Truth, and Grace - Pulsing with Light and Life.

GAZE UPON LOVE
LUKE 2

The Angel of the Lord appears to shepherds, in fields outside the village – they're guarding sheep. They were doing what they did each day, when a *SUDDENLY* took place. They were close, and yet without revelation or visitation, would not have KNOWN the Messiah was born. Close, yet so far away. The lost around us – He's At Hand – Yet, they do not see – they do not know He has come. Angel messengers - Sons of Light – messengers of the *Good News of Great Joy* - Behold the Light has come – the Light of the World.

You will know Him – HOW? Find Him in a manger, wrapped snugly in strips of cloth. Humble clothing - this One who left His Robe of Light, now wrapped in simple strips of cloth. You will not find a GREAT conquering King. You will GAZE UPON LOVE ITSELF - Perfect obedience - Perfect Love of Son for His Father. His *YES* made way for OUR chance to also respond to Love's Request for our hearts. They would GAZE at PERFECT LOVE. His CRY resounded in Heaven. Did angels dance - for the silence of the Second Person of the Trinity was heard once again? For those nine months, what did it sound like without the Voice of the Son? Did His Heartbeat in Mary's Womb echo THERE? Did it continue to be the Rhythm of Heaven?

The simple shepherds now surrounded with Heaven's Prophetic Song, sung by the Armies of Heaven - for they knew was their Commander, though a babe – was still the Lord of Hosts. They prophesied Heaven's Song to earth.

"Glory to God in the highest heaven and peace on earth to all whom God favors." Luke 2:14 (NLT)

Favored Mary
Favored shepherds
Favored Joseph

Holy Spirit Infilling *(Luke 1:15)* - John the Baptist, even BEFORE his birth. No limitations – who can tell God what to do? This baptism of fire from Above; this fire, this Presence was above and around all of the Israelites.

"The Lord spread out a cloud above them as a covering and gave them a great fire to light the darkness." Psalm 105:39 (NLT)

This Fire, now within Elizabeth's womb – within this child – yet to be born; He would come forth and be a blazing torch in the Hand of God. He was set apart with words of Truth – burning passion – preparing the way for the Bridegroom; a true friend – Friend of Holy Fire.

Oh, hear the Sound – the Sound of Mary greeting Elizabeth. John leapt within, and then Elizabeth was FILLED with the Holy Spirit. She prophesied of what she could not – did not know, "You are blessed by God among all women and your child is blessed. What an honor that the mother of my Lord should visit me. When you came in and greeted me, my baby JUMPED FOR JOY the instant I HEARD your voice. You are blessed, because you BELIEVED that the Lord would do what He said."

Jesus, a seed in Mary's womb, caused Elizabeth to bow in her heart and release prophetic decrees. As a seed, Divine Seed of Heaven, she postured herself and declared before His birth! Her eyes were opened; her heart understood by Spirit revelation.

Filled with the Spirit, the Baby jumped for Joy; even as all of creation would at His Birth. Do we hear the SOUND of Mary's greeting? What did she say? It still echoes in time.

The Lord sent her to Elizabeth to seal within her, with one on earth; one, who saw and heard - they would stand together when man did not understand. Impregnated by GOD, Mary would not only remember Gabriel's visit, but their face-to-face on earth visitation together. She would remember JOHN'S LEAP, Holy Spirit filling Elizabeth and her decrees over Mary. She had no tape recorder or scribe to pen it down;

it was penned by Holy Spirit on her heart. His Finger of Fire writing it and we read it today to remember. She would remember entering the house and greeting this other chosen womb. It would be a candid shot in her mind's eye and spirit, to call upon again and again. In the face of rejection, persecution, hard journeys, and no room in the inn, this moment penned by His Hand, on the tablet of her heart; forever BRANDED on her spirit! OH LORD, BRAND US with Holy Revelation, that in our darkest hours we remember SOUNDS – LEAPS IN WOMBS – DECREES – and we press into You.

5

Light & Life

IMMORTAL SEED WITHIN

"You have been regenerated (born again) not from a mortal origin (seed, sperm) but from one that is immortal by the ever living and lasting Word of God." 1 Peter 1:23 (AMP)

The Holy Seed Sperm – Jesus Himself is now within US. No longer mere mortals, we are a RACE that has never existed before – sons of God. We are holy, because He is Holy. As He increases in us through our daily dying, daily communion, we decrease. This Immortal Eternal Lord – The Word within us – *"Be holy for I am Holy!"* (Leviticus 19:2). Mary's Womb - Our wombs - Not tombs of hopelessness and despair, as are the lost without Jesus; as we were before this salvation...this SEED going in – born again into Eternal future and hope, we yield ever more to Him. We must see, and meditate upon this truth: We are not just men, but sons of God. We are not meant for just the ordinary, but the extraordinary supernatural realms of God.

He wants us to carry Him and birth His purposes, Noble purposes, Holy purposes; and see ourselves as He sees us. We are foreigners in this world. We do not fit, and we were never meant to fit. We are His offspring. He did not come into this world to fit in, but to transform; to bring Kingdom of Heaven to earth; to reveal His Father – His Home – Our True Destiny.

IMMORTAL SEED within us, what does this look like?

What comes forth from our lives –this seed within us, our DNA is the HOLY THREE. We must not focus on earthly fathers, mothers, or DNA with its weaknesses, failures, and generational curses, BUT ON OUR HOLY HERITAGE AND LINE - CHRIST JESUS IN US - Regenerated – truly born again – FULLY ALIVE with NO LACK – to live and move and have our being in Him! Because HE is in us and we are in Him, clothed WITHIN with LIGHT, Pulsating Light – wanting to get OUT. **"Let there be, let there be, let there be..."** pushing at the gates of our lives - mouths, eyes, hands, feet, hearts, and ears. Holy declarations of life giving Light and Life, pushing at the gates – *let us out*! BE RELEASERS OF HOLY LIFE.

It is not for the one next to you, IT IS YOU – young and old this day - IMMORTAL SEED WITHIN. Do you see it? Will you carry Him - Holy Ark – Holy Wombs? Feel HIM leap within you. Leap of DIVINE JUSTICE waiting to be released through Kingdom sons. Extending Him out of the gates of our lives; let the River flow out - River of Fire and Life. See it rushing forth – Holy Light - consuming darkness. You see injustice and release from the gates of our lives and spiritual wombs - JUSTICE, JUSTICE, JUSTICE, JUSTICE, JUSTICE! Five Piercings of Justice on the Cross - Now Risen in you and in me.

I'M YOURS!

"Prophetic Song of Zechariah:

Then his father, Zechariah, was filled with the Holy Spirit and gave this prophecy: 'Praise the Lord, the God of Israel, because he has visited and redeemed his people. He has sent us a mighty Savior from the royal line of his servant David…'." Luke 1:67-69 (NLT)

John, my little son, will be called prophet of the Most High. And why, what will this prophet do? What do we do as a prophetic, royal priesthood with a prophetic lifestyle call? WE PREPARE THE WAY FOR THE LORD! We tell people how to find salvation and forgiveness of sins, because God's Tender Mercy and Light from Heaven is breaking upon us AGAIN. Suddenlies – visitations to give LIGHT in response to our cries and decrees; to those who sit in darkness and in the shadow of death; to cry out for white light visitations - Holy Light to guide them (and us) to paths of peace – His Holy Promise - to the Mighty Savior King and His Kingdom.

"…to the wisdom of the upright (which is the knowledge and holy love of the will of God in order to make ready for the Lord a people (perfectly prepared in spirit, adjusted and disposed and placed in the right moral state)." Luke 1:17 (AMP)

Zechariah did not believe fully the angel, he was struck silent. His mouth opened again, when he obeyed and aligned himself with the prophetic word and mandate of Lord, "You must call his name John." When we WROTE on the tablet, his mouth opened, tongue loosed, and he began to speak blessing; praising and thanking God.

An AWE and REVERENTIAL fear
came on all their neighbors…….

Angels sent from standing in the very presence of God *(Luke 1:19)*. Oh, may we have ears to hear and eyes to see His holy messengers, as they come. May we receive what they say and not doubt.

"For with God nothing is ever impossible and no word from God shall be without power or impossible of fulfillment." Luke 1:37 (AMP)

MARY BELIEVED! (Luke 1:38 and 45)

We must believe what He speaks, and posture our spiritual wombs!

PSALM MEDITATIONS – HOLY ILLUMINATIONS

"You are the One who covers Yourself with Light as with a garment who stretches out the heavens like a curtain or tent." Psalm 104 (AMP)

Let Your Glory Surround Me, Let It Cover Me Like a Blanket

Surround me – clothe me in Light and Glory
Illuminate - Radiate
Let it break open the dawn –
Breaker of the dawn!

SPIRIT BREATH

"When you send forth Your Spirit and give them breath they are created and You replenish the face of the ground." Psalm 104:30 (AMP)

Breathe Out – Breathe In Resurrection Life. We are to be Life Releasers - He is in us. Womb of Birthing – Dance of Light!

"The ENTRANCE and UNFOLDING of your Words Give Light; their *unfolding gives understanding (discernment and comprehension) to the simple."* Psalms 119:30 (AMP)

YOUR WORDS come forth; You speak and breathe them from Your Throne. See them quick as lightning – flashing - coming through the gates and entrances of our hearts. And, unfolding His Garment of Light INTO US – AROUND US – THROUGH US - FILLING US with discernment, understanding, comprehension, and simple devotion – devoted Hearts.

"I OPENED my MOUTH and panted [with eager desire], for I LONGED for Your commandments." Psalm 119:131 (AMP)

HOLY DESIRE – HOLY LONGING, Entrance of His Commandments into our being. Breath of Light and Life, breathe IN – Open Wide – Eat- Drink – Breathe.

"For the god of this world has blinded the unbelievers' minds [that they should not discern the truth], preventing them from seeing the illuminating light of the Gospel of the glory of Christ (the Messiah), Who is the Image and Likeness of God.

For what we preach is not ourselves but Jesus Christ as Lord, and ourselves [merely] as your servants (slaves) for Jesus' sake.

For God Who said, Let light shine out of darkness, has shone in our hearts so as [to beam forth] the Light for the illumination of the knowledge of the majesty and glory of God [as it is manifest in the Person and is revealed] in the face of Jesus Christ (the Messiah).

However, we possess this precious treasure [the divine Light of the Gospel] in [frail, human] vessels of earth, that the grandeur and exceeding greatness of the power may be shown to be from God and not from ourselves." 2 Corinthians 4:4-7 (AMP)

Illuminating light of the Gospel of the Glory of Christ... God said, "Let light shine." Light shone in our hearts, so as to beam forth, the LIGHT for the illumination of knowledge and majesty, and the glory of God...We possess THIS precious treasure – DIVINE LIGHT OF THE GOSPEL!

"Our fathers in Egypt understood NOT nor appreciated Your miracles; they did not [earnestly] remember the multitude or Your mercies nor IMPRINT Your loving-kindness [on their hearts], but they were rebellious and provoked the Lord at the sea, even at the Red Sea. Nevertheless He saved them for His name's sake [to prove the righteousness of the Divine character], that He might make His Mighty Power known." Psalm 106:7-8 (AMP) *author emphasis.

Cause us to IMPRINT Your Loving-kindness on our hearts!!

YOU rebuked the RED SEA (Psalm 106:9).

Dried it up! You led them through DEPTHS, as through PASTURELAND. This was and is nothing to YOU. We walk on DRY PLACES, because ETERNALLY THE RED SEA IS PARTED! Jordan backed up to Adam. Death was swallowed up. Iniquity and curses forever demolished.

6

❧ ❧ ❧ ❧ ❧ ❧ ❧ ❧

Encountering Mercy

❧ ❧ ❧ ❧ ❧ ❧ ❧ ❧

FORGIVENESS AT HIS FEET

AT HIS FEET this woman found forgiveness and protection.
The council room of Heaven convened,
and Holy defense stood in the face of her accuser.
The religious spirits and the self-righteous bowed their knees and
walked away, for the One Who is Righteousness stooped before them,
writing with His Mighty Right Finger of Power –
releasing Mercy to the accused and challenging her accusers.
Light and Truth and Mercy
WON
What would we write?
Would we be dropping stones,
Or writing in the sand?
Do we stand between, or
Release accusations and judgments?
May we never be found accusing,
But standing in mercy and forgiveness -
Defending the accused with the Father's protection and love.
Jesus only did what He saw the Father doing -
Protecting His daughter and Jesus' future bride.

"Jesus walked up the Mount of Olives near the city where He spent the night. Then at dawn, Jesus appeared in the temple courts again, and soon all the people gathered around to listen to His words, so He sat down and taught them. Then in the middle of His teaching the religious scholars and the Separated Ones broke through the crowd and brought a woman who had been caught in the act of committing adultery and made her stand in the middle of everyone.

Then they said to Jesus, "Teacher, we caught this woman in the very act of adultery. Doesn't Moses' Law command us to stone to death a woman like this? Tell us what do You say we should do with her?" They were only testing Jesus because they hoped to trap Him with His own words and accuse Him of breaking the Law of Moses.

But Jesus didn't answer them. Instead He simply bent down and wrote in the dust with His finger. Angry they kept insisting that he answer their questions, so Jesus stood up and looked at them and said, Let's have the man who has never had a sinful desire throw the first stone at her." And then He bent over again and wrote some more words in the dust.

Upon hearing that, her accusers slowly left the crowd, one at a time, beginning with the oldest to the youngest, with a convicted conscience. Finally, Jesus was left alone with the woman still standing there in front of Him. So He stood back up and said to her, 'Dear woman where are your accusers? Is there no one here to condemn you?

Looking around she replied, "I see no one, Lord."

Jesus said, 'Then I certainly don't condemn you either. Go, and from now on, be free from a life of sin." John 8:1-11 (TPT)

HOLY SPIT

"As long as I am with you My Life is the Light that pierces the world's darkness."
John 9:5 (TPT)

THEN, Jesus spat on the ground and made some clay with His saliva. He is Light, and as He spit onto the ground, the very ground He spoke into existence; the ground became a tangible substance of heaven. All creation responds to Him; they know who He is – as the Father had shaped the earth into man and breathed into it – Light and Life, so Jesus spits – Holy Spit – even His spit is teeming with Life and Light - the DNA of heaven. The clay formed by Holy Spit and dirt, became healing clay, teeming with Light and Life. We were formed and shaped from dirt. We are clay in the Potter's Hands!

This man was born blind, so Jesus makes the clay, spits on the ground, applies, and anoints the blind man's eyes with the clay. Going back to the place of his birth – addressing the lack of sight - I AM applying the *Clay of Redemption* – beautiful prophetic symbolism! He did not sin, nor his parents. In that moment, we see a miracle of the Kingdom of God at hand.

A baby born without sight, now a man – blind all of his life, and the Creator of the Universe, Who took on the form of man, became a man in humble obedience to His Father's Desires, spits on the ground and makes clay and applies this clay to his eyes. Restoration and Justice stand in the gap – they fill in the missing piece. Blindness is swallowed up by the Light that pierces the darkness; not just spiritual darkness, but emotional and physical – every sphere impacted by the One, Who is Light!

He said, "NOW, go wash the clay from your eyes in the ritual pool of Siloam" (John 9:7 TPT). NOW – not tomorrow or the next day – don't go ask advice or the council of others, go NOW and wash (and no other location) – He was SPECIFIC!

"Or, 'the pool of apostleship'. Siloam is a Hebrew word that means 'to be sent' or 'to be commissioned'. The

Greek word for apostle or apostleship is the closest meaning. The apostle of our faith is the Lord Jesus Christ who was sent from the Father. To wash in the pool of apostleship is to recognize the healing that flows from the one who was sent from heaven" (Simmons, 2014, p. 55).

This man had to believe, receive, trust, and act upon the *specifics* Jesus spoke to him. *"So he went and washed his face and as he came back he could see for the first time in his life"* (John 9:7c TPT). Receiving apostolic authority from Jesus Christ, as Lord of all; obedience released, and acted upon brings forth healing and creative miracles - the blind see!

He invites us to wash our eyes in the Pool of Siloam, for we are to be sent ones, commissioned ones, whose eyes see clearly WHO HE IS! He has given us all authority and power to see our lives, callings, circumstances, dreams, and visions from His View – Heaven's View. There may be places of blindness in our lives that need to be washed off, so we can truly see. The blind beggar, now had eyes to see, and he would never have to beg again. His whole life was transformed.

We are not to live as slaves, our Father and Heaven's Promises and Provision are ours. We must see correctly and respond properly. We should no longer say, "If you want to heal me?" This man did not even ask, he simply reached out to Jesus.

Now his declaration and testimony is - "I'm the one who WAS blind. I am no longer blind; no longer a beggar. I met the man, named Jesus. He rubbed, he instructed; I went, I washed, and I began to see for the very first time ever." All action words - the God of action, Who moves on behalf of His children - we must engage with Him.

"A man anointed my eyes with clay, then I washed and now I can see for first time in my life." John 9:15 (TPT)

It was the ANOINTED touch, and the anointing on the clay from Hands of Light that healed him that day. It's the same anointed touch we need on our spiritual eyes to see afresh in this season!

"All I know is that I was blind and now I can see for the first time in my life." John 9:24 (TPT)

Religion and the law demands explanations – how, who, what? What about the laws and the guidelines? Did He have a name badge, go through training….who qualified him?

"You were born a blind, filthy sinner," the accuser and destroyer begins to speak, and they threw the man out. Religion will always accuse and judge. Self-righteous Pharisees will throw people out onto the streets, because they could not deal with the TRUTH. Jesus challenged the religious leaders with the TRUTH of FRUIT. TRUE LIGHT touched man's eyes and he sees. Who else has done this? This statement would challenge the leaders with the question of why this man had never been healed before this? Who else has done this?

Of course, if our hearts look upon a blind person and call him a blind, filthy, sinner, then we are filled with religion and self-righteousness. We would not care, nor reach out; we would walk by, accuse, and also be powerless to do anything.

Mercy always triumphs over judgment! Jesus learned they threw this man out, and He went and found him. The Shepherd's Heart seeks us, finds us, and pursues us. He asks this man, *"Do you believe in the Son of God?"*

"Who is He, Master? Tell me, so I can place ALL my faith in Him," the man replied.

"You're looking right at Him. He's speaking with you. It's Me, the one in front of you, NOW!"

The blind man's natural and spiritual eyes opened. Religious leaders could not see Jesus, but the eyes of his heart opened, along with his natural eyes. When Light touches us, we are touched in our whole being - DNA – body, soul, and spirit.

"Then the man threw himself AT HIS FEET and worshipped Jesus and said, 'Lord I believe in You!'" John 9:38 (TPT)

Posture of his heart – gratitude, adoration, worship, thanksgiving, and the faith of a blind beggar – now a wide eyed open seeing son of God!

"And Jesus said, I have come to judge those who think they see and make them blind. And for those who are blind, I have come to make them see. Some of the Separated Ones were standing nearby and overheard these words. They interrupted Jesus and said, 'You mean to tell us that we are blind?" Jesus told them, 'If you would acknowledge your blindness then your sin would be removed. But now that you claim to see, your sin remains with you.'" John 9:39-41 (TPT)

If we acknowledge our blindness, then sin can be removed. If we claim we see and sin remains, then we are truly blind indeed. Pride leaves us caught, trapped in sin. Humility opens the door and sets us free.

Open my eyes, Lord, where I am blind
Touch my eyes afresh with Your Holy Spit
I worship at Your Feet
I believe
I know only Your Touch of Light -
Illuminates the eyes of my heart and soul
Then, I see what I could not see

"The best way to live is with revelation–knowledge, for without it, you'll grow impatient and run right into error." Proverbs 19:2 (TPT)

EXTRAVAGANCE REVEALED

She poured forth perfume
Costly extravagance revealed
Why this waste?
She had caught a glimpse
A sliver of Light – Revelation
From sitting at His Feet
An understanding – This is the One
Who will waste Himself on and for – me!
And how can she do anything less
Than take what the world said was her security
and lavish it all
extravagantly on Him
Pouring forth
She declared in her actions
YOU are my security
YOU are more valuable than silver and gold….
I WILL waste myself on You
worshiping with all my *future*
And call it – SIMPLE DEVOTION
From a heart - that by Your very Spirit -
YOU enlightened and enlarged
Not for more things or for notoriety
But for YOU
Extravagance revealed
through the heart of one whose eyes had been opened
AT HIS FEET
She saw Eternity's Kiss
And she bent down and poured in grateful devotion
Man called it wasteful
The ONE whose opinion matters called it:
An eternal message of pure love
that would echo through time and space

Resounding over and over and over…
Here I am
Here I come to pour
To offer every part of me - everything else I ever trusted in
I ask for nothing in return
For I have had a glimpse of PROMISE
I see with the eyes of my heart
I know I can pour because
I am YOURS, now and for all of eternity
Extravagant SONSHIP revealed
Slavery within – crushed that day
Liberty and Love's Fragrance flowed
As an offering received and recorded in Heaven
The death of worldly security, the death of man's opinions
Extravagant worship
Captured His Heart in that moment
Preparing Him not only for His physical death on the cross
But the betrayal coming in the garden
One followed (Judas) – for political and religious gain
This one (Mary) worshiped just to be up close, again -
One more time AT HIS FEET
And her posture of being poured out
Helped prepare His Heart for the pain about to strike it –
Betrayal
Both had access to His Heart
Up close access
One entered in
The other stayed at a distance
Betrayed with a kiss
On the cheek
But Mary prepared Him with humble pouring
and kisses and tears
At His Feet
Extravagance prepared the way for betrayal's kiss
30 pieces of silver, versus Mary's *life savings*

Who do you say I AM?
You can only offer your all when HE is your everything
Extravagance revealed!

WHY THIS WASTE?

The religious spirit is still speaking this lie, both to and through God's people this day, over those who are lovesick. To those who are abandoned, who do not bow their knee to the fear of man, but choose to walk in the reverential fear of the Lord - their hearts and spirits do not care what men think, or the religious systems of our day, for they have an audience with the Lover of their souls, with the Creator of all. And, what can man possibly do or say to stop these ones?

They are not faint of heart, for their hearts burn with extravagant adoration. The words of the accuser that come like a flood to the flames in their hearts will have no effect, for the blaze upon the altar of their hearts burns brightly. They are filled with the oil of joy and gladness from being up close with the One Who is Joy and Gladness.

Their souls are filled with the words of His delight over them. When the waves of accusation and *why this waste* come to the shores of their souls, there is no place to come ashore, no place to land! Their whole being has been quickened, awakened, made alive, teeming and pulsing with Life Words, Light Words – they guard the perimeters of her soul – like sentries which declare, "NO ACCESS HERE!" No room in the inn of her heart! This heart and soul is full to overflowing with the goodness of the Lord, in the land of the living!

Sentries of light and life – the words of the Lord spoken to our hearts, souls, and our entire beings - radiate and exude the reality of **wasting ourselves** on Him!

HIS FEET

She smelled the nard and His feet
Up close - His feet that walked
dusty, dirty streets
Feet that soon would be pierced for her

She heard the repulsed comments of her accusers
She heard Jesus' comments also
To leave her alone
She would be remembered, always

She heard her own heart beating rapidly with extravagant love
She heard His heart beat also - responding with Merciful Love
She felt His acceptance of her love offering
It overtook the rejection hovering in the room

She saw Feet,
She saw Eyes of tender gazing love
She saw angry eyes, when she first came in from those in the room-
But chose where she focused
the Feet and Face of Jesus
Feet of Peace that would crush satan under them
Feet of a Man - Feet of the Creator - Feet of the Son of God
Feet of the King of Kings - feet of Flesh - Feet of Bronze

She kissed Eternity's Feet
The Eternal One
From whom all time came forth from
She tasted her encounter and experience of passion and compassion
Of tenderness and victory
She tasted of His pleasures
Intimacy with the One who loved
In broad view of the whole room —

so much for secret devotion
So lost was she - in His love - it became
The Secret Place

John 11:1 – Mary was the one who would anoint Jesus' feet with costly perfume and dry His Feet with her long hair. *"When Mary finally found Jesus outside the village she FELL AT HIS FEET in tears and said, 'Lord if only You had been here my brother would not have died'"* (John 11:32 TPT).

His Feet – at His Feet – a familiar place - a place of humble learning and eager hunger and expectation. She would set everything else aside. He was in the house – nothing else mattered – it could wait. A place of worship – kissing His Feet – preparing Him prophetically for His crucifixion and resurrection – adoring Him in holy worship.

She was a woman of surrender to His Love – abandoned love! So, when her brother Lazarus died and Jesus came, she fell At His Feet – the place she loved to be, and as she had done many times. His heart was moved.

"When Jesus LOOKED at Mary and SAW her weeping AT HIS FEET....He shuddered with emotion and was deeply moved with tenderness and compassion." John 11:33 (TPT)

He SAID to them, "Where did you bury him?"

Not only did she weep AT HIS FEET, but spoke words of total confidence in Who He was..."If only You had been here!" He had the power to stop the death and power to raise Him.

This whole story is filled with the emotions of Heaven!

"Then Jesus, with intense EMOTION came to the tomb... 'Roll away the stone!'." John 11:38a, 39a (TPT)

Compassion released the power of resurrection authority! Mary, who lived at His Feet in her heart, and displayed it in the natural countless times – moved His Heart with her tears. She moved the Father's Heart, for He only did what He saw the Father doing!

Martha was still talking about his body decomposing after four days – "Didn't I tell you that IF you WILL believe in ME you WILL see God unveil His Power!"

Reason or revelation? Unbelief or faith? Two different heart postures – only one brings us to His Feet.

"With a LOUD VOICE Jesus SHOUTED with AUTHORITY – LAZARUS COME OUT OF THE TOMB!"

Passion and compassion with Authority, declared LOVE'S REIGN of Father and Son over death. His Words rang through the atmosphere, releasing Lazarus from the grip of death. Words of Light and Life permeated his DNA, and Light overtook darkness. The DNA of Father in Heaven teemed into Lazarus's body, and death could NOT hold him – his body, soul, and spirit had to respond to I AM'S DECREE!

Those words are still moving through time and space. The decree of coming forth from death to Life! Physically and spiritually!

A woman's tears At His Feet – one who loved Him with a holy, reckless, radical love – moved Heaven – moved the Savior of the world's Heart, and the first resurrection took place. Holy Compassion revealed the Father's Heart!

7

❧ ❧ ❧ ❧ ❧ ❧ ❧ ❧ ❧ ❧

Eternal Decrees of Eternal Love

❧ ❧ ❧ ❧ ❧ ❧ ❧ ❧ ❧ ❧

LIFE AND LIGHT

"Life itself was in Him and this life gives light to everyone. This light shines through the darkness and the darkness can never extinguish it." John 1:4-5 (NLT)

May Your Light within
shine through
Darkness attempting to wrap me
In a cocoon of hopelessness and despair
May I break forth like an eagle from its perch to
catch the updraft of Your Spirit
I will be satisfied
to be the simple butterfly
struggling out of its cocoon
Transformation season coming to an end
For now…
Only let the cocoon
Unfold
It is dark and lonely in here
Could it be as the cocoon splits open
There the Light of You emanates
glowing Light - working within
a cocoon of circumstances
that had the appearance of destruction
death hung around - Grey
Yet colors within the cocoon – released -
Colors of transforming hope
Death to a caterpillar's
earthbound ways and thoughts
Coming forth - fluttering
Floating on winds of sound and color
From Above
Catching the wind of His Spirit

To live truly by
His Thoughts and His Ways
Earthbound no more - Soaring with wings of colors and light
Declaring - death where is your sting!
Oh painful cocoon time
So lonely - so grey
I await the release of soaring again
On colors and sounds
Stopping only to alight
For the fresh nectar of Heaven
Drinking of His Goodness
Resting on The Rock
Sipping on Living Waters from Above

Can you hear the sound of cocoons splitting open upon the earth? Like the stone being rolled back from Lazarus's tomb, there is a SOUND of cocoons splitting open and the power of TRANSFORMATION being released.

The season of waiting has come to an end; the hidden dream within the cocoons of our lives, in this season is now the time of release and birthing! The decrees issued from Heaven – as it was over Lazarus for him to come forth, are the same in this season over the Body of Christ...

My overcoming warrior lovers, come forth from the cocoons of being transformed into My likeness and soar, fly, and feed on the nectars of My Truth and My Love, now! This will strengthen you each day. Drink deeply of the nectar of My Love; and the joy that will fill you afresh each day will cause you to soar from victory to victory! You will not be weary as you feed on My Love and My Delight over you. Each flower is another facet of My DNA, Who I AM, and Who I AM within you. Drink of My very attributes – come and drink – and then, like the butterfly rest on the Rock in the sun and warm their wings - rest in Me. For I AM the Rock of Revelation, and in the Son's Rays of Light and Love, you receive revelation, impartation, and strength to soar from revelation to revelation. And, as you come together with the Body, you will feed each other with that which I have revealed to you, not for your edification, or for you to be applauded or recognized, but for My Name to be made great, and for corporate maturity into My Likeness.

Drink of the nectar of My Heart of Love. Drink deeply, for this is the power of the Cross. The very strength of your being, your inner man, and the courage you need in this hour and the days ahead – will be to drink here daily! This is the nectar of Galatians 2:20! The end time Bridal Army will have the fragrance of this nectar upon her, within her. It will be the song of her heart and the banner in her hand! She will dance the abandoned dance of holy love – dancing in the sky – over the earth – with the Lord of the Dance! Together, they will wave this banner over the Church – His Bride – and display the power of a life laid down in glad surrender to the One Who is Worthy!

The power of a laid down life brings forth a holy desperation within our hearts - desperate for more of Him, never satisfied, longing for more of His Love, more of being in union with Him. Not simply for the pleasures we receive, but so we can go out into the world and see as He sees, and reach out to the lost and desperate who do not know that what they are desperate for, deep inside, the longing, can only be found in Him.

When I am desperate, I know only one place to go, to the Feet of the One Who saw each situation in my life on the Cross; and gladly laid down His life. He would be the Eternal Answer for each circumstance in my life and heart.

HOLY DESPERATION

"Some men came, carrying a paralyzed man on a sleeping mat. They tried to push through the crowd to Jesus, but they couldn't reach him. So they went up to the roof, took off some tiles, and lowered the sick man down into the crowd, still on his mat, right in front of Jesus. Seeing their faith, Jesus said to the man, "Son, your sins are forgiven." Luke 5:18-20 (NLT)

While meditating on this passage, I began to see through a spiritual lens, as if I was right there viewing this moment of holy desperation. What does holy desperation look like - it looks like this!

They tried to push through the crowd to Jesus, but they could not reach Him. Holy desperation came upon them; they climbed up onto the roof, took off some tiles, and lowered their sick friend, who was still on his mat right in front of Jesus.

Seeing their faith, Jesus said to the man, "Son, your sins are forgiven." He didn't ask for his name, heritage, or if he fasted and prayed for 40 days. He saw faith in action – holy desperation. Holy covenantal caring - our brother cannot remain this way – there's healing in that place, we must get him there no matter what it takes.

In Luke 5:17 it says, *"And the Lord's healing power was strongly with Jesus."* It says He was teaching, but I believe that much more had to be going on for it to say this. I believe that as He taught, people were getting healed by His Presence, His Word, His Touch, and His decrees. And, suddenly a man drops down in front of Him – holy interruption!

He did not say, "Who interrupted My message?" For **HE was the message** and now, the Message would be shown again – declaring that He was the Lamb, Who forgives sin. He was the Healer, the Son of God! The Son of God calls this man – son! Not *hey you*, but son! "Son, your sins are forgiven." Decreeing who he was, and the action Jesus took in response to their act of desperation.

94

I AM the Last Adam and I AM the first born Son of God! You will be one of many sons who walk the earth – forgiven and healed. You will walk as a holy declaration, when the world asks, *"Who do you say that I Am?"* Your life and body will reveal to them – Jesus Christ is the One True God!

"Stand up – take up your mat and go on home."

"WHY?"

"Because you ARE healed!"

Immediately, he jumped to his feet while everyone watched. Can you feel the tension in the room, religious demons accusing Jesus of blasphemy, and Jesus saying He will PROVE that "I, the Son of Man have authority on earth to forgive sins?" Another Mount Carmel moment: religion versus relationship; law versus liberty; slavery to a system versus healing, wholeness, and forgiveness.

"Stand up take your mat and go on home because you are healed' was all that was needed. Holy Pure Heart of Compassion flowed with the Holy Oil of Healing. Words of Healing Love and Light from His Mouth and Being – this Holy One of Holy Life released wholeness with a command, not a suggestion! **Stand up!**

And then what do I do?

Take up your mat and go home. Take your mat that held you captive in sickness, roll it up, put it under your arm, and walk out of here healed. Sickness is no longer your master! Walk out and go home. SHOW the ones you love; the village you live in the Greatness of the Kingdom of God, the Love of the Father and Son, and the working of Holy Spirit. Never lay on that mat again. Display it as a reminder – son – forgiven and healed! Divinely owned, divinely forgiven and reconciled, divinely healed and made whole. All the privileges of sonship!

He immediately jumped to his feet, picked up his mat, and WENT HOME praising God, not staying for another touch for himself. OBEDIENCE – he BECAME the touch for the next person. As he WENT, he became the testimony for those who didn't or couldn't get to that house that evening. Jesus' healing touch EXTENDED through this man – now a son – nameless – what was his name – son, healed and forgiven – THRUST – SENT into the village – sent home.

Picture this – this one carried for years, now comes walking with his mat under his arm. The same streets that he has watched as he had been carried, turning his head one side to the next to see the marketplace activity - kids playing, dogs barking, vendors selling. Now, he walks fully upright looking, praising, and declaring with each step, "I am a son and I am healed and I am forgiven, so I praise the God of Healing Love." It says everyone was GRIPPED with GREAT wonder and awe and praised God over and over saying, "We have seen amazing things today."

ARE WE GRIPPED with great wonder and awe at the touch of the Master's Hand? This should *Grip Us* – for it is the Eternal Hand reaching, touching those He cares for. We cry out for more and we must, but in the meantime, each touch of a life, no matter how big or small, should bring great wonder and awe.

I made a trip to Ghana with Gateway Christian Fellowship in 2008. In the slums of Accra, our hearts were gripped with awe and wonder, as we saw again and again God's Healing Touch of Mercy and Compassion - open eyes, open ears, and open hearts to receive Him into their lives. He transformed hopelessness with future and a hope. I saw through the lens of Heaven, the children of God with hearts of simple faith. We lowered them before their Maker and asked for Mercy's Touch, and wept tears of joy as we watched Heaven touch earth!

At His Feet, there is always healing, always love, always grace. Holy desperation brings us to the Feet of the One, Who is the Answer for each desperate cry of our heart and souls; each desperate situation can be changed in a moment, at His Feet!

ONE TOUCH – FIVE WORDS
LUKE 5:12-13

Jesus met a man with an **advanced** case of leprosy.
This man **saw** Jesus, **fell** to the ground
face down in the dust begging to be healed,
crying out to him – "if you want to, you can make me well again…"
Jesus reached out and touched the man and Mercy responded –

I WANT TO - BE HEALED

INSTANTLY, this man's leprosy disappeared.

One Touch – Five Words – Five, the number of Grace!
A Recreative Miracle
A Suddenly of God
Touched this man's advanced leprosy of his
body – heart – soul
When Jesus suddenly comes – we must step into
HIS WORDS STILL SUSPENDED IN TIME

I WANT TO - BE HEALED

Step into the atmosphere of healing, released from His Mouth –
Creative Miracles – Resurrection Breath
Creating an Atmosphere of Divine Suddenlies
Oh
I WANT TO
Leper – clean
Five Words
Healing Breath
Suddenly Whole
Whole by Holy Breath
And Holy Words of Grace

Five Words – Heart of Heaven
Heart of Holy Three
I WANT TO - BE HEALED

The Great Eraser
Erasing every doubt
Of His Desire to heal
Erasing questions
Of why not yet

Step deeper into "I WANT TO…"

Face down on the ground, at His Feet, The Word spoke the healing words of grace and mercy! He calls to us to come closer, to let His Words of truth remove every question of doubt and despair. In those moments, when sickness has lingered too long, debt has piled too high, and the marriage has become too distant and cold, there is the invitation of Heaven to step deeper into His **I Want To** – heal, provide, restore – for I am the God, Who draws near – come a little closer!

EBB & FLOW OF HIS LOVE

At the shores of His Heart
I hear the waves lapping
At the shores of mine
Inviting me deeper
Ever deeper
Inside His Heart
Wave after wave of Eternal Love
Washing over
Washing into
me
Each wave depositing another portion of
Divine Holy Love
Another part of His Nature
Another removing of flesh
Replacing it with divinity
The ebb and flow
He increases
We decrease
From the place of rest and abiding
In His Heart
On the shores of earth –
Heaven's waves come and wash
Again and again and again
Holy waves
Glory waves
Depositing Radiant Light
Holy Fear
Reverential Hearts
Filled with awe for the Almighty
Who set the boundaries for the seas with His Finger
And yet sets no limits for our access to Him
How far and wide and deep we go

Depends on us
Purchased Access
Will we venture in?

Being at His Feet is not just surrender for surrender's sake, nor to lay down our lives for the lives of another, but it is His bidding us to come, that He may wash into us, wash over us afresh with His Love and Joy from Above.

There is always a choice to venture in or not - our choice. God sends wave after wave of refreshing love, pouring into our beings, the substance of His Love, that we may run with His Love.

We choose how far, how wide, and how deep we will go. Do we even dare take this journey? I say, "Yes – cast off every restraint – every fear – every inhibition and venture in." For this we were created, to live in the ebb and flow of His Love!

At His Feet, we encounter the footsteps of holy Love drawing near. This God we serve, this amazing all powerful Creator, reveals to us a love that stuns us, and causes our breath to be caught away. He steps out of Heaven to redeem us! The pride of man will often hold him back from posturing himself at the Feet of this King. Yes, the One Who is King of the Universe does not hesitate, even for a moment, the ultimate display of love and humility – One Eternal Step – toward you and me – to purchase for us – Eternity!

ETERNAL STEP OF LOVE

A decree of authority and humility, of promise and hope, of joy and salvation.

"A Savior has just been born in David's town, a Savior who is Messiah and Master. This is what you're to look for, a baby wrapped in a blanket and lying in a manger." Luke 2:9 (MSG)

Humility – you won't be looking for an earthly king, pomp and circumstance, emeralds and diamonds with servants and slaves. No!

But the King, the Messiah, the Master of ALL!

He will be found in a manger, a baby, once on a throne, now lying on straw in a trough. Humility at its highest expression, no other act of humility can compare...Humility born out of Eternal Love. "What is love," we ask? There it is for all mankind to see - the Eternal One steps down, leaving all of Heaven behind, taking it off as a robe. He steps out of the Heavenly Realms, down into a womb as a seed. He grows into a baby; a man child, and when it is TIME He bursts forth with Angelic Announcement. To who? To the simple shepherds on their night watch.

At the angels' decree, the angelic choir joins them singing God's praises, *"Glory to God in the heavenly heights, peace to all men and women on earth who please Him."* Luke 2:14 (MSG)

He was not wrapped in a royal robe or the moon and stars any longer, but a blanket, strips of cloth, swaddling clothes.

The angel tells the shepherds, "After searching, you will find a Baby – the One Who IS Christ the Lord. Not will be, but is!" He did not become Savior Lord as He grew, but before the foundations of the earth, He was and is and always will be. God could have sent Him as a full grown man to live, train up disciples, and lay down His life on the cross. No! He came as a seed, became a baby, born of a woman and

101

grew into a man with a father and mother on earth – with a heavenly Father and Holy Spirit in Heaven.

Two realms – Heaven and earth –
connected by this Baby – man child Jesus.

The angels, who came and sang, were not angels strumming harps with halos over their heads. This was an angel army of the troops of Heaven –*a heavenly knighthood* praising God. The first angel carried the glory of the Lord, and this glory flashed and shone all about the shepherds. They were terribly frightened. The Holiness of the Presence of Heaven touched down on earth. Here is reverential fear in action – down on their faces –in awe – trembling in His Presence.

Holy Heaven's Atmosphere suddenly appears to simple shepherds on their night watches. And, today they still come to those whom He chooses to send them to – night watches – day watches – holy encounters – as they wait. Those searching, actively looking will find Him.

The shepherds understood they needed to ACT on the word the angel had spoken to them. They said, *"Let us go over to Bethlehem to SEE this thing that HAS come to pass – which the LORD has made known to us."*

If our day was interrupted today – our calendar filled – our day planned out – and the angel came and spoke to us, what would we do? Would we drop all and go seek? The Kingdom of God has never been about convenience. What do we do when He speaks to us – gives prophetic word to us – do we act on it? What would we do if an angel appeared to us right now? What do we do with Divine Suddenlies, these Divine Interruptions in our daily lives?

It says they went with HASTE and by SEARCHING they found Mary, Joseph, and the Baby lying in a manger. Not any baby with a small *'b'*, but The Baby Who would be and always was the Lion and the Lamb!

Maybe we should be like the simple shepherds, who respond to Heaven's announcement – for all those who stumble in the darkness,

behold your Light has come! May we bow in holy reverential adoration
– God with us!

He is but a breath away, one glance of our eye, one whisper of our
hearts and He is there – God with us – Emmanuel! Master of all!

The Eternal Step of Love –
bringing Light and Love for all to see and receive.
Humility at its highest declaring –

Luke 1:78-79

*"Because of and through the heart of tender mercy and loving-kindness of our God, a
Light from on high will dawn upon us and visit [us]."*

*"To shine upon and give light to those who sit in darkness and in the shadow of
death, to direct and guide our feet in a straight line into the way of peace."* (AMP)

8

To Dream the Impossible Dream

WHAT IS SUCCESS?

What is success in heaven's eyes? This is the kingdom reality we must live in. The world pulls at the hearts of men to earn more and busy themselves. Success means working harder, more material possessions, and more friends. This is the tyranny of the urgent dictating the lives of millions. While He sits and waits for just one to come and rest, to sit at His Feet and listen to His Heartbeat, the Voice of Wisdom Himself!

THIS IS SUCCESS

To Wait
To listen
To abide
In HIS Heart
Bosom
Secret Place

This is success -
To drink of Him
Transformed into His Likeness
From here
Write
Worship
Pray
Dance

Create
From union with
THE WORD

At His Feet, He awakens dreams within our hearts. Dreams, the Holy Three placed within our beings even before we were born. When they convened and spoke us into existence from their holy Divine Council room, there were dreams that only we were meant to fulfill. Each of our lives so unique and diverse, not one alike, no one dream the same. Those nail pierced Feet were pierced and bled that we might fulfill Heaven's dreams!

DARE TO DREAM

God's House is called to be a place where each one's dreams can come forth. A place where our dreams are woven like a tapestry to bring forth God's corporate dream, and when He turns it over and reveals it to the world, they see Him and His Kingdom of Love.

We need to own those hidden dreams within our hearts, as well as those thoughts we thought were just our own thoughts. Why not you, why not now, it is never too late? We never want to live our lives with regret. We must be willing to make mistakes, arise from them, step out again, and learn from our mistakes. It is a journey. It is not so much about a destiny and destination, but a journey with God. It is so important to keep going, ever deeper into the dream He has put within our hearts. God Himself is the destiny and He is the journey; the One we journey with!

His Dreams do not come forth in isolation; they are linked with His body – family. We help bring forth each other's dreams. Being part of a family is a key for our dreams to become reality!

Matthew the tax collector, what was his dream? He was hated, despised, and called the scum of earth. There was no place of peace for him, until Jesus called to him – come and follow Me! Follow Me out of this place, into an even more difficult place, but one that is filled with My Glory and My Love. Suddenly he was accepted, valued - Jesus even went to his house to eat. Jesus' love and acceptance transformed this man's heart and life. Jesus gave him a dream - to follow Him. Once he was hated, now he was loved and called and would be sent. He now was part of a family and he could live in the joy of being celebrated instead of despised.

Mary and Martha had a dream that Lazarus would not have died if Jesus had been there. Jesus' powerful words would fulfill their heart's cry and dream:

Our friend Lazarus has fallen asleep, but now I will go and wake him up. Roll the stone aside, so they will believe You sent Me, Father. Lazarus, Come Out! Unwrap him and let him go.

These were not suggestions He spoke, but commands with all of the Father's authority and Heaven's power released, for the sake of the Father's Glory, and for the love of His friend.

Jesus has a dream that we will do the same to those who are asleep spiritually and physically. Roll away the stones of death - death of dreams and destinies. Prophesy to wombs ready to abort spiritually - Come forth! Unwrap the ones bound in lies and grave clothes of deceptions. Exchange for His Kingly robe, ring, and sandal – authority through His Love.

The Centurion pushed through everything for the dream of his servant being healed. Jairus had a dream for his daughter being healed. The woman with the issue of blood had a dream that caused her to push through every legality and religious boundary of her day, to touch the ONE, Who oozed Heaven's Healing Grace.

Jesus has a dream for friends. John 15:14 says, *"You are my friends if you obey Me. I no longer call you servants...a master doesn't confide in servants..."* Would we tell a stranger our secrets, invite them into inner circles? Of course we would not – neither does the Father, Son, or Holy Spirit!

"Now, you are my friends, since I have told you everything the Father told ME." He shared His deep intimacies, heart to heart, with devoted eyes, ears, spirits... "You didn't choose ME I chose you."

He appointed us to GO, and produce lasting fruit - SO THAT, the Father would give whatever we ask for using HIS NAME. And, give what is needed to produce lasting fruit. I COMMAND YOU TO LOVE EACH OTHER!

"Oh, there is so much more I want to tell you, but you can't bear it now. When the Spirit of truth comes, he will guide you into all truth. He will not be presenting his own ideas; he will be telling you what he has heard. He will tell you about the future.

He will bring me glory by revealing to you whatever he receives from me. All that the Father has is mine; this is what I mean when I say that the Spirit will reveal to you whatever he receives from me." John 16:12-15

TELLING YOU WHAT HE HAS HEARD
TELLING US ABOUT THE FUTURE
HE WILL BRING ME GLORY,
BY REVEALING TO YOU WHAT HE RECEIVES FROM ME

"I am praying not only for these disciples but also for all who will ever believe in me because of their testimony." John 17:20 (NLT)

GOD'S DREAM

"Jesus said these things. Then, raising his eyes in prayer, he said:
"Father, it's time. Display the bright splendor of your Son,
So the Son in turn may show your bright splendor
You put him in charge of everything human
So he might give real and eternal life to all in his charge.
And this is the real and eternal live:
That they know you,
The one and only true God,
And Jesus Christ, whom you sent.
I glorified you on earth
By completing down to the last detail
What you assigned me to do.
And now, Father, glorify me with your very own splendor,
The very splendor I had in your presence
Before there was a world
I spelled out your character in detail
To the men and women you gave me
They were yours in the first place;
Then you gave them to me,
And they have now done what you said.
They know now, beyond the shadow of a doubt,
That everything you gave me is firsthand from you,
For the message you gave me, I gave them;
And they took it, and were convinced
That I came from you.
They believed that you sent me.
I pray for them.
I'm not praying for the God-rejecting world
But for those you gave me,
For they are yours by right.
Everything mine is yours, and yours mine,
And my life is on display in them.

For I'm no longer going to be visible in the world;
They'll continue in the world
While I return to you.
Holy Father, guard them as they pursue this life
That you conferred as a gift through me,
So they can be one heart and mind
As we are one heart and mind
As long as I was with them, I guarded them
In the pursuit of the life you gave through me;
I even posted a night watch
And not one of them got away
Except for the rebel bent on destruction
Now I'm returning to you.
I'm saying these things in the world's hearing
So my people can experience
My joy completed in them.
I gave them your word;
The godless world hated them because of it,
Because they didn't join the world's ways,
Just as I didn't join the world's ways.
I'm not asking that you take them out of the world
But that you guard them from the Evil One
They are no more defined by the world
Than I am defined by the world
Make them holy — consecrated — with the truth;
Your word is consecrating truth.
In the same way that you gave me a mission in the world,
I give them a mission in the world.
I'm consecrating myself for their sakes
So they'll be truth-consecrated in their mission.
I'm praying not only for them
But also for those who will believe in me
Because of them and their witness about me.
The goal is for all of them to become one heart and mind —
Just as you, Father, are in me and I in you,

So they might be one heart and mind with us.
Then the world might believe that you, in fact, sent me.
The same glory you gave me, I gave them,
So they'll be as unified and together as we are –
I in them and you in me.
Then they'll mature in this oneness,
And give the godless world evidence
That you've sent me and loved them
In the same way you've loved me.
Father, I want those you gave me
To be with me, right where I am,
So they can see my glory, the splendor you gave me,
Having loved me
Long before there ever was a world.
Righteous Father, the world has never known you,
But I have known you, and these disciples know
That you sent me on this mission.
I have made your very being known to them –
Who you are and what you do –
And continue to make it known,
So that your love for me
Might be in them
Exactly as I am in them."
John 17 (MSG)

Hebrews 11 - Dreamers

They had dreams, many never saw, but they ran the race with faith, focus, and devotion.

TO DREAM THE IMPOSSIBLE DREAM!

Abraham offered Isaac. Noah built a ship on dry land. Abraham said, "Yes," to travel to an unknown land and lived in tents. He did it by

114

keeping his eye on the unseen city, with real Eternal foundation. A city designed and built by GOD. Sarah became pregnant and now millions are in Abraham's lineage.

Moses chose a hard life, over a simple and soft life with oppressors. Israel crossed the Red Sea, marched around the walls of Jericho. They toppled kingdoms and saw justice at work. They took God's promises for their lives, and were protected from lions, fires, and sword thrusts. They turned disadvantage to advantage, won battles, and routed alien armies. But their lives of faith are not complete, APART FROM OURS!

We must dare to live out the impossible dream that God has put within our hearts, from the place of His Love and His Joy flowing in and through our hearts! This is what causes us to push through every hindrance, speak to every mountain to be removed, and step into this journey and adventure of a life walking with God, living out the dreams He has put within our hearts.

"WHO WANTS ME, JUST FOR ME," SAYS THE LORD?

Who wants ME, just for Me?
This is His Heart cry to His people
Those who will seek Him for intimate relationship,
This is what Jesus died on the cross for,
Restoration of covenant relationship with the Trinity
Yes, we need to seek His gifts– BUT – seeking Him first
For relationship and then from this place
His gifts will come forth with holiness, purity and power
Flowing from oneness with Him

Who wants me, just for me?
This is the heart cry of His people to each other
Not wanted for their gifts, but for who they are
Heart to heart fellowship
Not being used for building a church or ministry
But pure and holy relationships that bring glory to the
Father, Son and Spirit

9

The Kiss of Eternal Intimacy

As we travel this journey with Him, we are transformed by being with Him. It is only from being with Him, that we are eternally changed. This is an adventure of how dead you can become, so that the risen resurrected King of Glory may walk the earth again through your abandoned life! Releasing true resurrection power!

DEAD MEN WALKING

The living dead
HE is more alive than you are
He has increased and you have decreased through adoration
The more of Him you want
The less of you exists
For HE overtakes you

Total annihilation of self
That He lives in and through every part of you
He - the Living One, in you
Radiates out
Permeates every particle of your being
This is how you can and will go through walls
Translate time and place
His Being overtakes yours
Weight of Him
Pulsating through you
His Power begins to overtake your hands
Feel His Life beating, throbbing in your hands
Let yours now be lost in
The Eternal One's Hands
Colors of soft green and purple hues
Soft colors and mingling of light and gold - soft amber gold
Encompassed in His weight and presence - you are
You want to live in this realm - relationship - always
Able to carry it longer and longer - to hover longer and longer

Until this is reality -
24/7/365!

What is our time worth? What is its value? Too expensive, too costly, too much time, too little time – excuses run rampant in our lives and society today! Time at His Feet, cannot, must not be forgotten or put aside. It is here we receive wisdom for our daily decisions, counsel for the situations we will soon encounter, revelation for the lives we will touch, and the kiss of Eternal intimacy for our hearts. When we don't have time with our King, others pay the price – that quick, cutting response, walking by the needy man on the street, or self-centered decisions.

OTHERS PAY THE PRICE

Others pay the price for our neglect of the Word and of quiet time
For only *here* are we truly changed – transformed
Into His likeness
When we stay away, our flesh will want to raise its head and
rule our soul
Others pay the price and we lose
Relationships
Time
Answers to our questions
We think we gain, but it's a lie –
We lose every time
We don't take time for Him
Not so we can feel better about ourselves
But because we will become a little more like Him and be
a living, walking blessing to the world around us

The art of waiting is almost nonexistent in our world. One minute of silence at a dinner table releases an awkwardness that screams, "Somebody speak! Somebody, do something, anything – just fill the silence with something!" The electronic age fills the silence with *clickity, clickity, click* - each lost in their iPhones, iPads, etc. They are lost in their own isolated worlds of electronic communications. How many friends do you have through social media? But wait, what is a real friend?

I remember a song I used to sing when I first met the Lord – *"What a friend we have in Jesus…"* I didn't fully understand it then, but I do now…Eternal Friendship with Jesus. Holy Spirit began to teach me and to woo me to wait at His Feet, wait to become like this amazing Eternal Friend, Who never leaves me, forsakes me, abandons me, betrays me, but is always there.

WAITING TO BECOME LIKE JESUS

There is a cry, deep within my spirit-man for greater silence; deeper places of God – hidden within – the mysteries of Heaven Above. There is still too much noise and busyness around me and within me. The goal is to pioneer the place of quiet and rest within the Heart of God. It is HERE, we are tutored by Holy Spirit how to live and move and have our being within the very Heart of God (Acts 17:28).

Once one accepts the Lord Jesus into their hearts and lives as their personal Lord and Savior, a transformation begins. We are no longer darkness, but light. We are children of the Father of Lights, from which every good and perfect gift comes down from Above. Jesus lives within our hearts and spirits – He is enthroned there. He is seeking to dethrone every place in our soul! This is where the noise is. This is where the warfare is – within our soul. He is seeking to rule our souls, and He does this one throne at a time. Whatever is above Him, or comes before Him that we have not given to Him, He is after.

For He is looking for a people, who are fully His – fully owned by Him – fully given over – gladly – from a heart of glad love given to the God, Who loves us wildly and passionately. The Celtic Church called Holy

Spirit the *WILD GOOSE* - none can predict His coming and going. So it is with seeking to live in this reality – it is wild and unpredictable what God will do, how He will come, and what He will ask of us. This is leaving the comfortable land of the familiar - even in the church - the familiar church service, the way things are done, and what we have come to expect...this is next and that is next; to break out into the place of abandonment to His visitation!

Even in the freest settings we fall into routines, and everyone seems to know what is next...worship, offering, announcements, maybe a prophetic word or two; a special song, the message, and then altar ministry. THIS IS ALL GOOD, but there is a way He is calling NOW - the *Wild Goose* is saying, ***"Will you leave the FAMILIAR and EXPLORE THE EDGE OF GLORY?"***

Leaving the familiar means we depend on Holy Spirit's unending creative release in our gatherings - both within the church walls and outside of them. Leaving the familiar however, especially in the church body, will lead us to people unlike us. They will worship other gods. They will not understand who you are and Whose you are, but this is one of the main reasons to explore, to reach a people with the Light of the Gospel of the Kingdom of God, and invite them to get into the boat of ETERNAL DESTINY and journey into our NATIVE HOMELAND!

This is not our home – this is our assignment. We are to bring Heaven down – to carry His Kingdom within us, and to release it everywhere we go. From this realm, we walk in a stillness and quietness within this noisy and restless world.

The world thinks they are pioneering, but often it is simply another gold rush - quick fix, self-centered, dog-eat-dog journey that ends in nothingness and emptiness! Only GOD can fill the void – HE IS THE JOURNEY and HE IS THE BEGINNING AND THE END. We begin *in* Him, journey *in* Him and *with* Him, and end *within* Him. Deeper and deeper, we venture into His Heart; into the realms of Holy Peace, Holy Light, and Holy Illumination. We will ride the waves of His Heart's emotions for us in our quiet times. Sometimes, still like glass. Sometimes, it is burning passion with wild waves lapping our heart and soul. This is the call to pioneer the emotions of God in quiet waiting and loving participation with Holy Spirit.

JESUS LEFT HEAVEN - HE IS THE ULTIMATE PIONEER - THE WAY MAKER!

COME SIT AT MY FEET

"Your attitude should be the same that Christ Jesus had. Though he was God, he did not demand and cling to his rights as God. He made himself nothing; he took the humble position of a slave and appeared in human form. And in human form he obediently humbled himself even further by dying a criminal's death on a cross. Because of this, God raised him up to the heights of heaven and gave him a name that is above every other name, so that at the name of Jesus every knee will bow, in heaven and on earth and under the earth, and every tongue will confess that Jesus Christ is Lord, to the glory of God the Father." Philippians 2:5-11 (NLT)

Jesus only did what He saw the Father doing, and He only said what He heard the Father saying. He lived this life before His disciples; they watched and observed Him day after day for three years. He set the example of going up the mountain, tarrying and praying in the garden, sitting by the sea – listening.

And, His Voice calls to us each and every day, *"Come, sit at My Feet – listen and consider what I have to say – here you will be forever changed!"* It is here, our hearts begin to surge with prayers from deep within our being that we did not even know were there. He awakens the prayers of our souls and brings them forth, poured out at His Feet, that He may respond.

As I waited with Him, meditating on two passages, a river of prayer began to flow from my heart and through my pen; I invite you to join your hearts with mine in this prayer…

LISTEN AND CONSIDER
MEDITATIONS ON ISAIAH 51:1 & PSALM 40:2

"Listen to Me all who hope for deliverance, all who seek the Lord, consider the quarry from which you were mined, the rock from which you were cut." Isaiah 51:1 (NLT)

Listen to Me...

Holy Spirit, open my ears to listen and to hear. I ask for ear-ways to be opened fuller to the Voice of the Lord, and to Heaven's activity - To be able to hear clearly, with no deception. *"Father, clear ear passageways,"* is my heart's cry! Holy Fire in my ears - cleaning out old wax- familiar - where lies have hidden and settled in - melt them today with fresh warm oil; the oil of Your Words of Truth. Cause this wax to disappear and fresh passageways, entryways, large canals with *Entrance for Truth only* - posted at the gateways of my hearing. May I not listen or agree in any way with any lie. May I not open my mouth to agree with anything, except what is holy, true, and righteous. Cause me to hear my own words that have agreed with the whisper of the enemy's lies, and to cancel them, to not speak them. I declare Truth only in my inward parts and in my ears.

All who hope for deliverance...

Lord, I hope for deliverance from every lie and false concept, every place I'm held back or hold back. I listen for YOU, and hope for Words of Life to bring deliverance in any area of my heart, mind, soul - that my spirit may be whole, and that I may live and walk in holy wholeness.

All who seek the Lord...

That I may search for You, and seek You with all of my heart and all of my being. That I would not grow lukewarm, but possess a fresh hunger and desperation to be with You, to know You, and to live in the depths and mysteries of Your Word. To be consumed with hunger beyond anything I have ever known. I ask for a searching heart, that I may find the depths, the heights, the width and breadth of You; Your Heart, Your Kingdom, Heaven, and Heavenly Places.

Consider the quarry from which you were mined, the rock from which you were cut...

The quarry of Your Heart, the Rock of Your very Self, Your very Existence; Quarried from Heavenly places, from within Your Heart and Being, from Your deep desire for a people to have intimate relationship with. Precious stones - to reflect Your Beauty, to reveal what Heaven is like - from places of the Deep - therefore Deep calls unto deep. Water of Your Word and Words still speaking to us - You quarried me from Your Heart - You call me a living stone to be used for the building of Your Kingdom.

You separated me from the large mass of rocks. Your huge, all searching, all knowing Hand of the Master Builder came and removed me. You set me apart from the pile of rocks of circumstances and lies that had become my place of residence. Hurling rocks of accusation, too weak from the many blows; they became piled high, and there I resided - in the mass of rocks of empty promises, broken dreams, wounding words, dark lies, shattered heart and soul.

YOU PULLED ME OUT

Placed me on the Rock and placed me in the Rock and declared me Yours (Exodus 33:21-22 & Psalm 40).

A stone hewn by Your Hand - from before time - known in the Heart of Father; Quarried with exact purpose and place in the Blueprint of Heaven - at this hour - decade - generation.

A stone of great worth,
because of the Quarry from where I came
A Rock from which I was cut

Rock of Christ Jesus -
Royal Rock
Royal stones

Silenced in the past by stones of rejection

STONE WHO ACCEPTED ME and quarried me, causes me to cry out with a loud voice -

I am a precious stone - precious gold - to be and reflect His Beauty - His Glory - the Heavens Above

And, I will not let the rocks of the earth cry out, due to my silence — No, I will open my mouth and speak of His Wonders.

I will let YOU continue to shape and chisel and make me into the perfect rock for building Your holy purpose - Your holy blueprint - your holy temple.

"He drew me up out of a horrible pit (a pit of tumult and of destruction), out of the miry clay (froth and slime), and set my feet upon a rock, steadying my steps and establishing my goings." Psalm 40:2 (AMP)

You mined me and set me on the Rock of Hope! You have put a message of future and hope in my heart and mouth, and send me out as a miner. To seek for precious stones, to dig for precious metals - those who are Yours and those who You are calling to Yourself. To separate, even that which is within, that is precious, from defilement. For, we are mined from Your Holy Heart's Quarry and cut from the Rock of Salvation. We are therefore invaluable - beyond measure. Who can measure the price - put a price tag on us? Who can label You Jesus, and all You are - or Father, or Holy Spirit or the Heavens? You mined us from WITHIN and You alone can say, *"YOU ARE MINE."*

TWO MARY'S
MARY OF BETHANY (LUKE) & MARY MAGDALENE (JOHN)

At His Feet, these two Mary's poured out their lavish worship by anointing Him with costly nard and perfume.

"Greetings," He said, and they ran to Him, held His Feet and worshipped Him."
Matthew 28:9

Here before them was the Resurrected One. They knew His Face, His Voice, and His Feet. They saw Him, they heard Him, they touched Him, and they smelled Him and tasted Eternity's Promise - five senses awakened.

They held His Feet - the Feet of Good News.

Feet that walked into hell itself, and took the keys back that Adam had surrendered.

> First Adam -
>> Stumbled feet - tripping over the trickery of the devil's evil schemes.

> Last Adam -
>> Pierced feet - purchased legal right of ownership for mankind once again.

>> Permission to use keys given to those who *hold His Feet* and embrace His Feet of Good News, Feet of Triumph, Feet of Grace and Mercy, Feet of Longsuffering and Love; Holy Feet, Warring Feet, Tender and Terrible Feet.

>> Hold His Feet and worship Him - posture of humility and adoration.

Beginning of fulfilling the Great Commission and obtaining the use of the keys.

Pierced Feet - pierces hearts of the simple worshipers - pouring in His Heart of sacrificial love and extravagant grace.

10

❧ ❧ ❧ ❧ ❧ ❧ ❧ ❧ ❧

Dawn Awakeners

❧ ❧ ❧ ❧ ❧ ❧ ❧ ❧ ❧

DO YOU SEE WHAT I SEE –
DO YOU HEAR WHAT I HEAR

An army of God's people are arising with fiery love and devotion in their hearts and eyes. They are fearless and focused, and their ears are listening intently for their Commander in Chief's Voice. They know who they are, and Whose they are. Because of this confidence in His Divine Ownership of their lives, they follow and serve Him from the place of compelling love.

The enemy of their souls fears the One, Who is in them. The understanding of this is growing more real to these ones each and every day. The reality that the risen resurrected King of Glory resides within their very spirit-man. That the One, Who conquered death, hell and the grave; the One, Who holds the Keys of the Kingdom is within their very being.

They release a sound when they walk, when they are on the move – a sound that causes Heaven to rejoice and hell to shake. It is the sound of His authority being wielded through His people. Those who look like Him, sound like Him, have His character and nature flowing through them. It is a sound of the Keys of the Kingdom jingling with Kingdom Releasing Power, as they move through their daily lives. These keys release the sound of **freedom and release** for every place of captivity in every man, woman and child's life, and propels them into their God-given destiny.

"God gave Paul the power to do unusual miracles, so that even when handkerchiefs or cloths that had touched his skin were placed on sick people, they were healed of their diseases, and any evil spirits within them came out." Acts 19:11-12 (NLT)

I believe there was a sound that emanated from Paul's handkerchiefs and the pieces of cloth when they were sent out. All who were willing to receive the anointing that flowed from these pieces of cloth, were recipients of Jesus' healing power. It was the power of the sound of the **Keys** being released, and was heard in Heaven and hell alike. Paul had come into the reality of Christ's Resurrection Power, into the reality of

"Christ in you the hope of glory" (Colossians 1:27), and it sounded like keys in the spirit realm – keys of the Kingdom in a piece of cloth. Can you hear it, can you see it?

Can you hear the sound of rejoicing and celebration, bodies healed, prayers answered? Can you see the joy on Jesus' Face, as one of His own steps into the place of sonship on earth with access to Heaven's dominion power? Not for their own name to be known, but for His Name to be glorified. When the piece of cloth touched Paul's flesh, it was touching the *organic union* of Jesus within his spirit, emanating His full authority through a man's body, and transferring it onto a piece of cloth. Where Paul could not physically go, pieces of cloth went – carrying the fullness of Christ's resurrection glory!

Can you see yourself walking into Starbuck's, your place of work, your home, your school – how about your church? Can you hear the sound of keys jingling from the spiritual belt around your waist? Can you hear those who have gone before you, cheering you on from heaven's courts? Can you hear the sound of prison doors of people's hearts opening, chains falling off of hands, ankles, necks; minds being loosed from oppression, depression, and hopelessness? Can you hear the sound of Kingdom Authority within you crying, *"Let Me out? Let Me Out?"* The One, Who is within, wants to be loosed into the marketplace through your life and mine. Do you see what I see? Do you hear what I hear?

I have felt this power and seen this power released in my *pieces of cloth* – flags, fabrics, banners – used in kingdom dance and intercession – releasing His Kingdom mandates from heaven on earth. It is not just for the book of Acts, this is for here and now. The Dancing Warrior King was simply looking for someone to let Him out! Will that be you? And, the exciting part is this: what will it look like being released from you? The sound will be the same however - the Keys of His Kingdom Authority!

"To them God willed to make known what are the riches of the glory of this mystery among the Gentiles: which is Christ in you, the hope of glory." Colossians 1:27 (NKJV)

"I pray that your hearts will be flooded with light so that you can understand the wonderful future he has promised to those he called. I want you to realize what a rich and glorious inheritance he has given to his people.   I pray that you will begin to understand the incredible greatness of his power for us who believe him. This is the same mighty power that raised Christ from the dead and seated him in the place of honor at God's right hand in the heavenly realms. Now he is far above any ruler or authority or power or leader or anything else in this world or in the world to come. And God has put all things under the authority of Christ, and he gave him this authority for the benefit of the church. And the church is his body; it is filled by Christ, who fills everything everywhere with his presence." Ephesians 1:18-23 (NLT)

"As a result, I can really know Christ and experience the mighty power that raised him from the dead. I can learn what it means to suffer with him, sharing in his death, so that, somehow, I can experience the resurrection from the dead!" Philippians 3:10-11 (NLT)

AWAKEN THE DAWN

Awaken the dawn with resurrection power
Dawn of resurrection morning
Teeming with the power of I AM
The Resurrection and the Life and the Light
I AM LIFE – I AM ALIVE
Awaken the dawn with a song
The thrush's song
Dawn awakeners
Sing the thrush's song out into the night
And watch
Awestruck as dawn arises
Before your very eyes
Believe – only believe
I AM is arising in the song of the dawn
Over the land
Over the lives
Of those you release the thrush song for and over
Hear it and release it and believe it

Kissing His Pierced Feet, she receives the thrush's song and sings out into the night - a song of the dawn - a song of resurrection release. These are songs of purity and holiness, with a sweetness that swells up from the heart. This is one who is not looking to be seen or noticed, but to release songs of the dawn - songs of life.

Thrush Songs

"Many people consider thrushes the most beautiful sounding songbirds in North America. Birders describe their songs as 'airy', 'flutelike' and 'haunting'. Each species of thrush has a distinctive pattern to its song. The Hermits 'Thrush' beautiful haunting song begins with a sustained whistle and ends with softer, echo-like tones, described as oh, holy holy, ah purity

purity eeh, sweetly sweetly. It pauses between each phrase and the song is about 1.5 seconds long. Hermit Thrushes also deliver an extremely faint 'whisper song' in spring" (WildMusic.org).

These songs rush forth from our being, awestruck as dawn arises; the wonder of a new day, a fresh grace, unlimited divine possibilities spread before us – our only limitation is what we place upon ourselves. This song of the heart awakens the dawn with a call to adventure and exploring the realms of God and His Creation, joining in creation's song of abundant life and heavenly wonders. The songs of holy, holy, holy; purity, purity, purity; sweetly, sweetly, sweetly – releasing songs of heaven's atmosphere.

Awaken The Awakeners

Time for another great awakening
He's awakening the awakeners
Those whom He quickens with cry of, "Awake, oh Sleeper."
AWAKE, AWAKE, AWAKE – AWAKE, OH SLEEPING BRIDE
Get yourself ready for harvest – THEN, the Bridegroom comes
Yes, get lovesick for the Bridegroom, so that what HE asks of you –
You will do – where He sends, whatever He bids –
Awake oh Sleeping Bride to His Desire of you
CONVINCED of THIS – you go forth in garments of acceptance
Loved by the Lover of your souls
Gladly you go where no man has gone before
Physically and spiritually - pilgrimages – mandates of Heaven
To release the CALL - AWAKE - AWAKE OH MY PEOPLE
AWAKEN TO HIM
As His lover, you then will go into harvest fields for HIS PROMISE
HIS REWARD – others, yet to be lovers
Those yet to be sons
And those waiting as you go prepare
the calf, robe, slipper, and ring
of ownership of Glad Love – Of a Glad Lover
Mad with love over those He died for – arose for –
Promised lovers of God waiting in the harvest field
Dry bones…passionate lovers
Awakeners come forth
Angels of revelation come and remove sleep seeds from our eyes –
Remove the stupor and awaken Your Bride
To SEE HIM and see lost lovers waiting to hear and know Him

The season of sleeping and being self-absorbed is over, and the season of the harvest is at hand. It is a mature Bride, who will arise and venture out into the fields ripe and ready to be harvested. This is not a project or a *to do list*, this is the heart of God and His Kingdom. This is why Jesus came and hung on a cross and rose from the dead. We are to awaken the dead places within our own lives with the truth of His glad and wild love for us. We are not to be an army of dry bones, but to become an army of passionate lovers; ones who are unstoppable, because we understand who we are and the mandate that is upon our lives as His lovers.

We do not live with an orphan heart of rejection, self-pity, and self-focus, but we look up and we look out with the Father's Heart. We celebrate each and every life that enters into the truth of sonship through divine encounter, and we participate through preparing the calf, the robe, the slipper, and the ring of divine ownership!

Being Awakened

Eyes to see, ears to hear, hands begin to feel and touch,
tasting of His delights,
smelling Jesus up close and near
Each vibration of Heaven can be experienced,
releasing transformation life
Shedding cloaks of shame - blushing red
For robes of righteousness and acceptance
Holy intimate attire - bridal pure by the Blood of the Lamb
Ownership - "thou art Mine"
Produces total trust and freedom from fears
Unshakeable confidence
because He has proved Himself in our tests and trials
Life is dancing over us again
Wisdom is playing its song to us calling us to arise and take our place
Come out of busyness, trying to prove our worth
The endless cycle - endless monotony
Come into LIFE and celebrate with HIM
Hear His heartbeat of love and passion
as you lay your head on His Breast
Look into Life's eyes and receive Resurrection,
Holy CPR into your being
Feel Holy Spirit rising in you- you are freer, freer, freer…
Strength surging into your soul and spirit
Casting off distractions
Taking Life's Hand - empowering you to walk in - Divine Exchange
Wisdom is celebrating now
The One from Whom all things exist-
Now angels join in - holy chorus of voices, tones, sounds
Calling you upward - shafts of light and tones showing the Way
To see His glory, hear His desires,
feel His pleasure, taste His goodness,
Smell His costly sacrifice

Holy Spirit is
Awakening our five senses

This is not an awakening for a moment; it is not awakening from a dream, turning over and then falling asleep again. This is every part of our being, every one of our five senses responding to His costly sacrifice, to His delight in us, and it impacting our spiritual DNA. It is the Holy Hands of a Loving Savior, performing holy CPR on our hearts, and releasing His resurrection power and life into our beings. New strength, new vision, fresh hope fills our beings, spiritual lungs and limbs.

Suddenly, we can see with the freshness of spring in our eyes and hearts. Anything is possible! We see, hear, feel, taste, and touch His goodness; we are undone – we are awake! We will not go to sleep again; this is our hour, this is why we were born, this is our season, and this is our day! No more holding back, no more looking back, we live present–future. The past is behind us, and all that attempted to hold us in the captivity of yesterday!

DAWN'S LIGHT

Foggy mist of morning
just before dawn
Awaken oh Bride
Awaken for the dawn is almost here
the night is almost over
Sing the ancient songs of those gone before you
chant with the birds of the air
declaring simple trust
in Me
Foggy mist of morning
dawn is approaching
announcing
Bright Sun just ahead
Sing the song of morning light
I am the Bright Morning Star
I arise just as dawn
awakens
dawn is just ahead
Bright Morning Star releasing
songs of dawn's light

He invites us to sit with Him in the mist of the morning. So often in the Bible, when we read of Jesus' day. It says, *"At dawn!"* There is something about the dawn. It is new and fresh and untouched – the sounds of man have not infiltrated the space of creation with the distraction and annoyance of man-made machinery.

It is sitting at His Feet, we listen with Him in great joy of heart to the songs of the dawn and join in with this glad celebration – announcing together – see the Bright Morning Star. I am at His Feet, and yet, HE is Above me, below me, around me, within me, and there is no place I can go that I am ever alone. He is always and forever with me.

Therefore, I put my full trust in Him. The safe place of being at His Feet is my dwelling place of eternal adoration, now and forever.

I join with the birds' song in the morning - joining in the ancient songs of those gone before us, who knew this place. If you listen deep within your spirit, you will hear from within and without the songs of the lovers now seated at His Feet in Heaven. Together we sing the ancient and new songs of the dawn!

HEAVEN'S RESPONSE TO EARTH'S PRAISE

There is a rumbling – can you feel it in the ground? It is the sound of the Body of Christ arising. It is the sound of the nameless – faceless ones coming forth. It is the sound of dry bones being renewed, strengthened, and refitted by His Hand, with His purpose – not by man's hand, nor for man's purpose. They are being made fit for Kingdom purposes in this hour.

It is the hour to put our ear to His Breast in the posture of intimacy. It is the hour to put our ear to the ground, and listen for His response to radical praise, abandoned worship, and kingdom declarations from earth. For as He responds to them, He sends forth His earthquake and His lightning from Above - like Paul and Silas in the deep dungeons – hands chained, they SANG A NEW SOUND OF WORSHIP when in captivity, for their spirits were not captive only their physical bodies.

They carried within their beings the
SOUND OF FREEDOM and LIBERTY.

They carried within their beings the
SOUND OF RESURRECTION POWER.

They sang a song in the night, in the dark, with chains….

They released notes and proclamations, and GOD IN HEAVEN HEARD and His response was one that caused a SHIFTING in the earth. It caused the response of BURSTING THROUGH AND BLASTING OFF CHAINS! It was the shifting from captivity and bondage put on them by religious men and religious systems – into the enlarged place.

GOD SANG HIS SONG back from heaven and caused the earth to shake, the chains to fall, and salvation to begin within the dark dungeon - out into the homes of the prison guards. And, it flowed into the marketplace; for God's Sounds are violent and they bring action with them!

The Spirit of Illumination – Holy Spirit – illuminates our hearts and minds, and causes us to hear and perceive and makes our steps clear. Our steps become steps of light, leading the way through the darkness.

God stomped His Foot in rhythm with the song and sounds of Paul and Silas – **Foot of Light** – releasing lightning – thunder – quaking and rumbling. These Heaven to Earth Sounds were Breaking open and Breaking through all religious captivity. No one would stop those who were His. He would join in and respond – THIS SINGING RADICAL LOVING GOD would show forth what a Holy Dance will release. It releases sons of God from every place of captivity, into His Holy purposes and plans!

Time for the Pioneers to come forth and lead the way!

Pioneering hearts and spirits, those who will not settle in the land of the familiar, come forth. These ones do not live complacent lives, but sit at the Feet of the One, Whose Heart burns before them. They warm their hearts and hands in the Fiery Heart of Love of their God. His red hot love of desire burns away any excuses, fears, and reasoning in the mind that would hold them back from venturing into the unknown territory ahead.

The cry from their lips is, *"Break camp! Fill in the ruts of the familiar, and let's break open new ground."* They will blaze a new trail, a new way, a highway of holy love; and they will be known as fearless, faith-filled, having been up close with the One, Who is Fiery Passion and Love!

11

❧ ❧ ❧ ❧ ❧ ❧ ❧ ❧ ❧ ❧

Journeying Into His Heart

❧ ❧ ❧ ❧ ❧ ❧ ❧ ❧ ❧ ❧

NEW FRONTIERS

Pioneering
Tear down the wagon train
Circled in complacency and safety
Around fires of
Warmth of the familiar and known
Break Camp
For I don't want a people who sit around the familiar fire
But I want to fill you with the Fire of Love –
Passion – Desire for Me and
My Heart's Desires
To break camp and dare to believe for New Land
New Anointing –
New Frontiers
I call you to the Frontier of My Heart
Undiscovered Country –
Unfamiliar Places
To be those who will venture into the Unknown
And find all that you thirst and long for
Yes, fellowship is good
But there is a time to come and explore
Deep Chasms
This takes coming apart
To diligently seek Me and My Heart
Let me take you Up and In
Not all those you know will come
Even those with years of relationship
But it is My Voice Calling Out
COME UP HERE
My Heart Crying Out
I STAND AT THE DOOR AND KNOCK
It is I – The Lord inviting you to come
And learn of Me – Be with Me

To let Me reveal Hidden, Deep Things
I want to show you
Will you leave the safety of the campfire
To become a people
Who burn like a Blazing Inferno
For ME
And all they touch will be impacted by
My Fiery Love and Glory
Will you be a people of who it is said –
THEY HAVE BEEN WITH GOD

Our being with God builds within our spirit a sure foundation of holy trust in the One, Who is trustworthy! We no longer hesitate between two opinions, two roads – we set our feet purposefully and intentionally upon the path of adventure. We are unshakeable in our convictions and immoveable in our faith. This again, has come from sitting at the Feet of the One, Who alone is the Rock of our Salvation and the Immoveable Mountain of Eternal unchanging love!

IMMOVEABLE MOUNTAIN

You alone are the Rock - the Sure Foundation
There is not one speck of sand we step on, stand on -
when we stand on You
You are totally Trustworthy - for You are all Truth
And therefore - ALL TRUST
When I put all of the weight of my life, my heart, on You -
It does not give way - nor shift beneath my feet
You are Steady and Sure and therefore as I am on You
In you - I am secure
For you will not change position
You swallow me up in the midst of a quake
You support and undergird and hold every part of me
On You I can walk and dance and leap and know
that I know, that I know
You are the Immoveable Mountain
The God of all the mountains and of all creation
I sit secure on You - in You - I choose to trust You!

Our hearts and steps are sure and steady, because we have taken the time to build a firm and solid foundation in the realm of our souls. We will not be moved, shaken, blown by every wind of doctrine that comes our way, or tossed by every storm that we encounter. We will be steady, fixed, and focused, because we do not journey alone. There He is the Faithful and True One, Who is with us.

Knowing that we have said, "Yes," to pioneering, and are secure enough in His Love to now move forth in a more mature love – He invites us into a pilgrimage journey. Many receive this invitation - not all say, "Yes." It will require dying to self even more. The flesh will cry out, "But I already thought I was dead." However, on this journey, it is where we are being transformed even more into His likeness – the goal always being – to be like Him in every way.

What will be your response? I believe deep inside of you is a pioneer waiting to burst forth, or at least, go where you have never been before.

PIONEERING NEW HORIZONS

Our Christian life is meant to be an adventure – to be lived fully in every way! God calls us to pioneer new horizons in the natural and spiritual realms. God never meant for our lives to be boring. He invites us to explore the wide open plains of His Kingdom, and to seek the *thin places* with Him. The *thin places* are where the heavenlies are more accessible, where Heaven and earth seem to kiss in extravagant ways, and we have the privilege to access and enter into the realms of Heaven. It is where we can hear His Voice more clearly, see from God's Eye View more clearly, and feel Him more intensely – a place with Divine Access! These are places where God's children have prayed and worshiped, and created a sacred space of intimacy with God for themselves and others to enter into the depths of God's Love.

Thus began my journey – I was born a pioneer – beckoned to blaze a new way. He brought me into a three year journey (and beyond) of studying the ways of Celtic Christianity. This led me to a pilgrimage to Scotland – Iona – Hebrides Islands. There, I encountered the thin veiled places, and met with God in unique and powerfully intimate moments.

The Lord called me to this pilgrimage, and put within my heart a blazing passion for this region - to walk in and experience these realms, this lifestyle – this prophetic journey. Also, to call and believe for an awakening that took place on the Hebrides Islands from 1948 to 1952, where the people of those islands were awakened into revival, which shook the islands with Holy Fire Visitation of the Lord.

I believe it is the *now* time of God to have our eyes opened to truly see Him and His Kingdom. As men and women, we can set borders and boundaries around our lives and our Christian walks. The Lord drew the boundaries of the seas and lands with His Mighty Finger, and yet, He invites us to step past our securities, ideas, and safe places; and step across our borders into the reality of *"In Him we live and move and have our being"* - for this to become reality – tangible – every moment of every day.

It was the cry of the heart of Celtic pilgrims – *"We see with the eye of vision even greater vistas, deeper relationships are waiting to be revealed. So we need to become explorers, that the vision of our world and ourselves may be extended. We need to discover the reality of our existence: to know who we are and to Whom we belong"* (Adam, 1990, p. 6).

Today, may our eyes be touched afresh as the Celtic Church understood and prayed:

"May the Lord Jesus touch our eyes, as He did those of the blind. Then we shall see in the visible things those things which are invisible" (p. 7).

They understood Creation pointed to a Creator. They saw creation as a way to commune with Holy Three – Father, Son, and Holy Spirit. All of creation worships Him; and if we are silent, the rocks will cry out! For too long, the new age movement has taken what has belonged to the Lord and His people - to hear the Lord in the wind whispering, to hear His Voice on the waves calling to our hearts, and to sing with the birds in the morning and awaken the dawn with a song.

God didn't create the earth and galaxies, full of its wonders and simply walk away, but He reveals Himself to man again and again. This God, Who is ablaze - He invites us into His Blazing Heart – to walk intimately with no compartments.

Our lives are not to be broken down into compartments where we change *hats* for each part of our day. Now, a father or mother; now at our job; now, a pastor; now...NO, it is walking in the ebb and flow of oneness with Him in all we do, knowing He is in us. *"To live and move and have our being in Him"* - throughout the day - an ebb and a flow of walking by His Spirit.

We need to regain a sense of wonder and reverence and awe! To walk in the wonder and awe of God!

"He encompasses us on all sides, like the world itself. What prevents us from enfolding Him in our arms, only one thing, our inability to SEE Him" (p. 8).

Celtic Christians did not seek to separate things in their world, but to ALIGN and bring them into unity. When they said, "Be Thou My Vision O Lord," they were asking to reach beyond what the natural eye could see – horizons and stars – to see the Creator Himself – to see the very center of everything! *"Open my eyes that I may see the WONDER all around me"* (p. 13).

Where there is no vision the people perish. I feel our vision is far deeper than what our call is, our church, or ministry. It is the vision of the Holy Three; to ever live within this reality of their tangible Presence – drawing near. Then, will we be aware and step in? It comes softly, gently - a cloud appears. Will we see - will we step in?

Celtic prayer was always for *Vision of God;* a God in their midst, Who encompasses them. God who was at their fireside, in the stable, walked with them, and watched over when they slept. No compartments - an ebb and flow - a rhythm - a lifestyle! This is not what American Christians, for the most part, experience. They are lost in iPods, iPads, noise, busyness, cellphones, texts, computers, televisions, more noise - daily life filled with noise and distraction. No stillness.

No journey of rest, little seeing and hearing, microwave Christianity, and microwave results - spiritual food that does not sustain – no quiet within – restless – always searching for satisfaction - the next word, the next place or thing.

May we pray as the Celtic saints did - that our eyes would be opened, and all five senses awakened to see His realm; to encounter the thin places and walk closely with Him; to walk in an expectancy to see Him, as they walked through their day. They walked purposefully and intently – gazing for Him!

It is all about the posture of our hearts – our inner beings – the very center of who we are - to live from our hearts.

They sought heart to Heart relationship with the Holy Three. They would not give up until His Heart was within theirs, and they were in the very Heart of God - pilgrimage of His Heart!

"Through the heart relationship, the vision is cleared
and all things seem to speak of God" (p. 23).

When I am not in this place, I do not truly see the butterfly's path; hear the bird's message in its song, or sense His Wind on my face and His Breath on my neck. I am not as quickened to the suddenly of **He is near!** I miss the dew lights' message on the grassy fields, sparkling with a chorus all its own; the sea and stars grand orchestration song and display; the Big Dipper extending to all who are thirsty – come! Orion – the great Warrior King, standing guard and watch over us! To stand at the shores and sing in the spirit from my heart, and release unto Him holy songs – knowing they go out – never to be stopped!

Even as *"Let There Be Light"* is still travelling through time and space - the Eternal Word - new galaxies are being created by His Eternal Decrees. He is in us. We are co-laborers – lovers – releasing the reality of His Kingdom. We must see and live, in and by and through the Heart of God. The Kingdom of God is within – Heart and heaven are one. Jesus is enthroned in Heaven and in my heart. It is here heaven and our hearts become one! Ever journeying deeper!

STAY IN THE CENTER

Deep, deep within, so deep
I heard His Voice speak
Stay in peace,
walk in peace

How Lord - I cried?
Walk in peace - stay in peace by staying in the Center

Do not let the enemy draw you, pull you to the outer realm
The circumference of the soul
Stay in the Center
Do not be pulled out
Stay - abide - in the Center
For within that place is ME
Words slide off
Arrows can't find you
You become untouchable to the enemy's plans against you

Stay in the Center - In Me
Transforming Light in the Center
Burning fires of orange and gold of My Passions
To get hotter - ever hotter- as you dwell
In the Center

It is important as we journey to stay in the Center. We cannot allow the enemy, our own soul, or the voices of well-meaning men and women around us to pull us off course. It will often be a fight to stay in the center – it is the center of His Flame of Love, and here is where anything that is not like His Nature is burned up! If we will remain, stay, abide - we will become what our own hearts' cry out for – a man or woman with His heart of passion.

Remaining in the center allows us to never lose our perspective or wander off the path, as we journey through wilderness seasons, respond to His calls of visitations up the mountain of transformation, or venture out into the sea of mankind with the power of His resurrection upon us and within us.

The One, Who is the Mountain behind the mountains - is the Chief of Mountains - beckons us to the foot of the Mountain, where His very Presence dwells. We ascend the mountain of holiness and burning love – this is the mountain of transformation.

This is the mountain of stillness, where we are taught to wait and to listen in silence before our True and Living God! Here is where Jesus would speak with His Father. Here is where He learned to wait and listen and come down the mountain and be about His Father's heavenly business. The gospels are filled with Jesus' divine appointments, which did not catch Him by surprise, for He only did what He saw the Father doing and He only said what He heard the Father saying! He and the Father were one, and He lived to please the Father.

It is from this place that we too will come down the mountain living to please the Father. We will see the needs of the people and respond with the Father's responses. Because we have been with Him on the mountain of His Presence, we will answer the cries and questions of the people, who wait at the foot of the mountain with a declaration of holy faith - **He Can and He Will!**

NEW SONGS FROM HIS HEART

Songs of His Heart
Flowing through yours
Notes of varied colors

Pink – compassion
Gold – glory
White – holy
Red – fiery passion
Yellow – joy

Weaving intermingling
Opening up hearts, minds, spirits
To realms and mysteries of God's Love

He invites you to explore realms of worship
You have not yet entered into
Deepest chasms and caverns of hidden mysteries
Waiting to be discovered and released
Will you mine the places of His Heart of Love with Him
Will you let them then go deeply into yours
to transform, renew, deepen
Beyond your wildest dreams
The reality of walking in His Amazing Love

As it cultivates deep within your spirit, it will shape, transform and
illuminate your mind and soul and whole being
Songs will come forth like rushing waterfalls over a high sea cliff
Misty sprays of joy will drench you and everyone in its reach
Inviting others to jump into the pools of holy love encounters

Songs from His Heart to yours
Priceless, costing Him everything, given to you freely

First and foremost because of His Love for you
Then for those people, places and appointments
where He will place you to release
That which has now taken root deep within
From this place the sounds and songs
will release the rivers of Passionate Love
From Heaven to earth
From His Heart to and through yours

There will be no limit, how high, how deep, how far you can explore
And release the songs of His Heart!

This love is deep and causes us to reach out past our own wants, needs, and desires. Now, we must share with others. It is not demanded of us, it flows from the realms of mining His Heart of Love with Him. We are not alone; we have been invited into a pilgrimage, a journey into the very depths of God's Heart.

This poem was actually written as I waited with the One, Who Is Love - sitting at His Feet for a precious Christmas gift – a word from His Heart – for her. This poem, I now share here with all who will read this book - as He extends this same invitation to you!

The deeper we venture, the more we enter into the reality of the riches and truths of truly experientially knowing His Love. We cannot hold this to ourselves; we are compelled from within our own spirits to bring forth praise and thanksgiving.

When a people, a body, an army of lovers begin to arise, awaken, and release the sounds of the dawn, declare His praises, and pour forth His love there is a response in heaven. Creation awaits it, groans and longs for it, and Heaven is ever watching and listening. Is there a people, who will sing a song from the depths of My Love that the earth itself will respond? I believe if you are reading this book you are one of those!

The songs that come forth are dangerous and violent in holy love! They cause the earth to quake and hell to shake, for it is the song from within the very Heart of God! The cry of freedom and release, the sounds of chains crashing to the ground, the brightness of His illuminating truth – all released in lavish praise. Songs of destiny and courage, of the price to be paid – willingly, gladly – swirl into the atmosphere. Angel armies join in. They have been waiting for what seems like an eternity for these sounds and these songs that release them to their commission in the heavenlies and on earth! Heaven's response to earth's praise!

UNCHARTED REALMS OF WORSHIP

He issued to us – an invitation to enter
The uncharted realms of worship
We entered not knowing where He would lead
Where He would take us by His Spirit

The four winds blew
The angels were present
The weighty Presence of the Eternal One
God of Eternity, Wonder and Majesty came down
His Breath among us, filling us afresh…
Breathing in Life and Light
Songs birthed by His Spirit
Aligning our hearts with heaven
Heaven in our midst
Holy, Holy, Holy
Moving with creation's dance and song
Holy Light surrounding…Holy Embrace surrounding
Imparting into our spirit man
Holy desire, Holy fire, Holy love
Rhythms and sounds of thunder

He wrapped us in His Divine Embrace…it sounded like thunder
Wrapping us in Holy Light – shielding, hiding, sheltering…
Sons and daughters of holy light and life…
Wrapping in His Desire…what more could one ask for
This God of Love filling our hearts
Bring us again into these uncharted waters of worship
The very river of life and fire pours in and through us
Bring us again into the unknown realms with You!

At His Feet

APPENDIX

The following Bible translations were used within the writings of this book. All scripture is used with permission by the authorized publisher. Scripture that is not marked by a specific translation is paraphrased by the author. Accents within scripture references are made by the author for emphasis.

∾ Scriptures marked TPT are taken from the following books of The Passion Translation:

 ∾ *Luke and Acts: To the Lovers of God, The Passion Translation,* copyright © 2014. Used by permission of BroadStreet Publishing Group, LLC, Racine, Wisconsin, USA. *(www.broadstreetpublishing.com)*

 ∾ *John: Eternal Love, The Passion Translation*^{TM}, copyright © 2014. Used by permission of 5 Fold Media, LLC, Syracuse, NY 13039, United States of America. All rights reserved.

 ∾ *Letters from Heaven by the Apostle Paul, The Passion Translation*^{TM}, copyright © 2013. Used by permission of 5 Fold Media, LLC, Syracuse, NY 13039, United States of America. All rights reserved.

 ∾ *The Psalms: Poetry on Fire, The Passion Translation*^{TM}, copyright © 2012. Used by permission of 5 Fold Media, LLC, Syracuse, NY 13039, United States of America. All rights reserved.

 ∾ *Proverbs: Wisdom from Above, The Passion Translation*^{TM}, copyright © 2013. Used by permission of 5 Fold Media, LLC, Syracuse, NY 13039, United States of America. All rights reserved.

∾ Scriptures marked AMP are taken from the Amplified® Bible, Copyright © 1954, 1958, 1962, 1964, 1965, 1987 by The Lockman Foundation. Used by permission. *(www.Lockman.org)*

The following references are found within the various writings of this book, and are noted as in-text citations. The below references are listed in order as they appear in the text.

❧ Simmons, Brian (2014). *John: Eternal Love, The Passion Translation*^{TM}. Commentary (p. 55). Used by permission of 5 Fold Media, LLC, Syracuse, NY 13039, United States of America. All rights reserved.

❧ Wild Music (n.d.). *Thrush Songs.* Retrieved on November 19, 2014 from http://wildmusic.org/en/animals/thrush.

❧ Adam, David (1990). *The Eye of the Eagle.* Triangle SPCK, Holy Trinity Church, Marylebone Road, London NW14DU.

ABOUT THE AUTHOR
DONNA MILHAM

Donna Milham is the founder of Eagle & Dove Ministries and Judah's Roar Church. She is a teacher, speaker, writer, and creative artist. Donna is called to train, equip and release people to know God's blueprint for their lives, and to embrace and fulfill their God-given destiny with passion and perseverance. She believes our lives are to weave a tapestry of God's nature and character for every eye to see and every ear to hear the goodness and greatness of His Name.

To learn more about Donna Milham, please visit *www.DonnaMilham.com*.

For more information about Eagle & Dove Ministries and Judah's Roar Church, please visit *www.eagledove.com*.

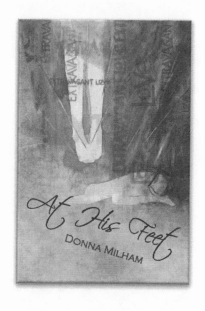

At His Feet

To order more copies of this book,
or other products by Donna Milham,
please visit *www.DonnaMilham.com*

Made in the USA
Middletown, DE
21 January 2015